WISHCRAFT

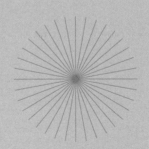

This book is dedicated to my mother, who passed
before it went to print. May she know how much her
invincible spirit inspires me to be better everyday and
in deep gratitude to her for instilling the courage in me
to live life true to my heart.

To my father for being a true friend. I am in deep
gratitude to him for sharing with me his practice
of prayer and patience, for always believing in me,
encouraging me to write a book and follow my dreams.

To both of them for showing me that in the end,
with enough compassion, perseverance and love,
dreams do come true!

SHAUNA CUMMINS

WISHCRAFT

A GUIDE TO MANIFESTING
A POSITIVE FUTURE

Hardie Grant

BOOKS

W.I.S.H.

Healing and change

What do you wish for?

Identify any resistance to recieving this and resource it with healing thoughts and feelings using your imagination.

Soften into the resistance with compassion. Befriend and collaborate with the parts of you that need healing or encouragement.

Harmonise and heal the resistance. Imagine yourself healing and responding differently to the old resistance or limiting belief.

C.R.A.F.T.

Change and transformation

C ollaborate with yourself
with compassion.

R eframe the problem with new
possibilities and perspectives.

A ffirm it with your words and mental images,
take action in the direction of your dreams.

F eel it as if
it already is.

T ransform positively
and patiently.

WHAT
IS WISH
CRAFT?

What is a wish? 11
My journey to WishCraft 16
Self-hypnosis:
   Your mind is a wishing well 22
Manifestation:
   Your imagination
   is a magnet 25
Changework:
   Life as a cosmic spiral 31

THE
FOUNDATIONS
OF WISHCRAFT

History, symbols & mythology
   to inspire your wishing 43
Wishing traditions
   from different cultures 48
The pillars of WishCraft 53
Simple steps to finding
   your wishing mind 60

Part V: Wishing Journal 136
Afterword 150
Acknowledgements 152
About the author 154
Index 156

WAYS TO WISH

THE WISHES

The overview effect 65
Cultivating your practice 67
Wishing rituals 83
The wishing hour 90
Everyday wishes 93
Wishing with friends 96

The wishes 103
Invocation:
  Relaxing, releasing
  & receiving 106
Wishes for healing 109
Wishes for giving 115
Wishes to receive 120
Wishes for different
  stages & phases 125
Wishes for revolution 129
Wishing hour:
  Deep mind wishing 132

I.

WHAT IS WISHCRAFT?

WHAT IS A WISH?

Hello, dear wishes.

Yes, that's right – wishes.

In the beginning, we were all wishes. When you think about it, it's quite literally true: we are the result of an act of desire. The word 'desire' comes from *'de sidere'* in Latin, meaning 'from the stars'. Humans have been wishing on stars, wells, wishbones, candles, eyelashes, flower petals and fireflies (among many other things) since the beginning of time. Across all religions and spiritual schools of thought, there is an active practice of petitioning the divine through prayer, meditation, trance, prostration, song and dance. Wishing has been an integral part of my spiritual practice since childhood, yielding many unlikely successes and glorious adventures, but it wasn't until I began the study and practice of self-hypnosis that I really began to master the art and enjoy the benefits of well-wishing (positive ritualistic wishing) and WishCraft.

In *WishCraft*, I will share the story of how I came to this practice. I will show you the ways in which I have learned to work with wishes and sometimes – against the odds – even make them come true.

By understanding self-hypnosis, both as a natural ability and a tool, we can learn to empower our wishes with intention. The energy of wishing is both primal and divine, and we can work with wishes as if they are a blessing, affirmation, meditation and prayer all rolled into one. By doing this, we can retrain the mind to focus, find and receive what it's looking for. Not only does this enable us to better believe in our ability to change or manifest but, most importantly, it can expand our awareness to notice and possibly attract positive experiences and opportunities that move us in the direction of our dreams. In other words, it can increase our ability to (as I like to say) 'surrender to the supportive forces within us and around us'. It also helps us, very practically, to make our wishes come true! This is WishCraft: the art of integrating self-hypnosis into the mystical world of manifestation, in order to organise our desires or wishes into action.

In my work as a hypnotist, I have shared this method with thousands of clients, witnessing them successfully train themselves to take control of their subconscious minds and make their wishes become a reality.

Throughout the book, I will include instructions and explanations on how to use wishing as a total mind, body and spirit energetic upgrade, by way of self-hypnosis. When we learn the art of well-wishing and the benefits of the 'wishing state of mind' (page 60), our subconscious mind becomes a proverbial wishing well: an ideal place to plant our wishes and watch them grow. A wish can act as a focusing lens for our desire, a portal for divine intervention and an energetic arrow to move us into action. The motto I want you to adopt as we dive in together is ...

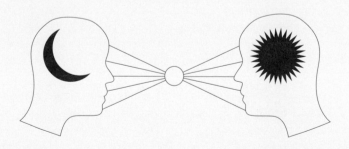

PERCEIVE.

BELIEVE.

RECEIVE.

I'm so excited to share with you my musings on the divine energy of wishing; the history, mythologies and explanations that have inspired me, and what the very human phenomena of wishing a wish actually is; and how I have used WishCraft illustriously in my own life to weave wonders and transform self-depreciation into self-collaboration and a compassionate mindscape. I will also teach you how to make your mind a 'wishing mind'. This process involves letting go of who you think you are and accepting that your capacity for change is greater than the conscious mind can realise. There will be detailed instructions for calming the mind in order to allow your wishes to influence you on a deeper level, as well as information on how to create an ideal environment for wishing, and how to adopt daily practices that will help your wishes come true.

My wish for you is that you get better and better at wishing well for yourself and the world, as you learn more about how your mind works – and how to make it work for you.

Repeat after me three times:

Just as I wish well for myself, may your wishes come true.

Just as I wish well for myself, may your wishes come true.

Just as I wish well for myself, may your wishes come true.

MY JOURNEY TO WISHCRAFT

Before I go into the history and art of wishing, I would like to share the story of I how I came to understand the idea of WishCraft. I hope hearing about my own journey to WishCraft will help you as you start out on yours.

It happened suddenly. I woke up in the middle of the night, after tossing and turning, my heart throbbing, anxiety pumping through my veins. As I lay there, adjusting to the darkness of my room, I thought: *WishCraft*. That's what I had been dreaming about: that's what my mind (and body) had been trying to tell me. The idea of WishCraft was born out of a sort of dream: a trance-like, insomnia-induced haze.

At the time, I was recovering from a particularly destructive relationship. It had left my nervous system completely shot and my head in a shambles, so much so that the trauma had caused sudden hair loss or alopecia, resulting in a complete bald spot on the top of my otherwise very thick head of hair. But that night, despite the unanticipated bald spot, was different. The thought of WishCraft woke me up like a long-lost, burning flame of desirous life-force energy: a last-ditch effort from my psyche. It told me it was time to do more than make lemonade out of lemons. It was time to make my dreams come true, once and for all.

What my dreams had revealed to me that night was profound, but in many ways, it was also obvious. *WishCraft*. Of course. That's what *it* was, that was what I'd been doing: what had helped me ever since I was a kid; what I did now, professionally, as an adult. But now I had a name for it. WishCraft.

It's what I did when I was sick as a child in my hospital bed, as I lay healing in an incubated tent, breathing through strange and debilitating inflammatory reactions as my skin flared up in wild rashes and my lungs contracted from pneumonia. I *wished*. I wished myself, my lungs and my body well. I wished it obsessively, as sick kids often do. I managed to channel my OCD in a positive direction of sorts, focussing my efforts on wishing. This calmed me, even as my body was on fire, fighting all sorts of things that the doctors didn't quite understand.

My brother had come to visit. In my memory it is like a movie from the 1980s. I think he arrived at night, after taking the bus up from college. I was the youngest of five kids, and he was the second oldest. When he was thirteen and I was still tiny, he had been tasked with sharing a bedroom with me, finding himself taking care of a crying baby. Like me, he had suffered through a lot of illness and many long hospital stays during his own childhood.

Now, stepping off the bus from college to visit his sickly seven-year-old sister, he brought me a plant. I believe it was some kind of clover-like plant, one that opened in the day and closed at night. Our parents are from Ireland, and we had a family habit of incorporating Irish mythology and culture into almost everything we did: blessings and rosaries decorated the house, copper-plated leprechaun statues sitting on pots of gold were tucked in hidden corners and beneath stairwells. Prayers and blessings and the idea of luck were always close to the heart and home, and so my brother let me believe that it was a lucky plant, a sort of wishing plant: that I could make wishes on it and that they would come true. And I did. I wished on it. I wished for my lungs, I wished for my heart, I wished for the other kids at the hospital to be well, I wished that one day I would grow up and be free, travelling to far-away places, writing in cafes along riverbanks, dancing into the night, finding whatever I was looking for.

And so, I cultivated this state of wishing and I let it drive me. Sometimes it drove me too far (for example, into the aforementioned destructive relationship); but sometimes it drove me right to the front door of what I wanted. Fast forward to twenty-five years later: I was in my early thirties, living in New York City, and I found myself becoming a Clinical Hypnosis Practitioner. Suddenly all the dots connected, and I realised that I had been hypnotising myself back then in that incubated tent, using the power of imagination to wish myself well and calm my system, and perhaps to help my healing. And now here I was, waking up that night in my bedroom from a strange, trauma-induced insomniac haze, to find the flame of my life force fighting hard not to be extinguished under the weight of my sorrow and self-pity, reminding me, once again, that I could organise my desire into action.

It was almost as if a voice had whispered to me (with a dash of Hollywood movie-like drama): 'Wake-up! Call this what you now know it is: WishCraft. Teach it as self-hypnosis: it's what you have been doing for years. Teach it in groups and ceremonies, through performance art and sound installations. Use it to make your wishes for art and collaboration come true and share it with others so that they can do the same.'

This realisation bolstered my confidence, enabling me to reach out and collaborate with people I admired and to take chances on bringing a creative project to life. This is a chance I would never have taken before. Within six months, I went from being avoidant and terrified of public speaking to performing live in theatres around the world in a hypnosis-inspired sound experience. This is just one example of how opening up and remembering the power and potential of wishing can launch you like a rocket in the direction of your dreams.

As I began to look back and reflect on how WishCraft had informed my life, a constellation of events began to appear to me in a meaningful pattern. When I'm asked about how I became a hypnotist, I often remark that it was like one of those moments when you suddenly realise that all the roads you have been following have been leading you to this path. And that is also true of the WishCraft.

In fact, my motto, 'Perceive, Believe, Receive', revealed itself to me when I realised that healing must come first. I remember a spontaneous healing that happened when I was 18 years old. I was travelling by bus through long stretches of American highway, watching the sunset and becoming entranced by the flat lines of the horizon. I found myself drifting into a dream where I met my inner child, or little Shauna, in a field not unlike the one outside the bus window. I experienced a moment of simple yet profound healing, where I hugged and deeply comforted my little self. However basic and unremarkable that sounds, it seemed to have a lasting effect on me. Looking back now, with an understanding of hypnosis, I can see how that spontaneous healing allowed for a new source of inner support to appear in an otherwise blocked-off area of pain. With this new reference for compassion and healing, my inner child was able to grow up with the support of my adult self. This healing gave me the reference point for safety and support that is so necessary for believing and receiving. First I had to perceive the healing. Then I worked to reinforce it with new positive experiences and references, so I could believe it. Then I was able to fully receive it.

Simply put, this moment of inner healing allowed me to create an internal sense of safety, which enabled me to take chances in the direction of my dreams, and it continues to grow and support me in taking risks. If things don't work out, I am able to trust that I have always got my own back.

It was this sense of safety that allowed me to take a chance on moving to New York City with $800 to start a magazine with two friends. I called on this strength when I imagined the actress who I wanted to appear on the cover of said magazine, and soon enough her agent reached out to us. I called on it when I fantasised about working as a hypnotist on some sort of tropical island; shortly after, I was asked to be the resident hypnotist of a summer-long art and wellness island festival. While on an artist's residency last summer, I wished to write a book about wishing; I was soon connected to a book publisher. This publisher had been reading a book on manifestation and had fallen asleep the night before we connected thinking: 'We need a modern version of this.' Fast forward one year, and *WishCraft* was on its way to publication. Which all sounds pretty magical, doesn't it? But engaging with this mythical process of perceiving, believing and receiving is actually something we are all born knowing how to do: we are co-creating our life experience with every thought that we think and every action we take, but WishCraft makes this a conscious, teachable system that allows you to get really good at it!

WishCraft is, in a very real way, a dream come true. It is my method of combining self-hypnosis practice with the practice of manifestation, a sort of special, mystical mix of 'Change the way you look at things and the things you look at change', and 'If you create it, they will come'.

WishCraft is available to all of us, in every moment of every day – we just need to know how to use it.

SELF-HYPNOSIS: YOUR MIND IS A WISHING WELL

In ancient Celtic traditions, people would go to the wishing well and surrender their wishes and their worries to the gods who dwelt in the water. During my hypnosis sessions with clients, I realised that there was a common thread between these early traditions and my own practice: as people entered a trance-like state, their subconscious minds became an ideal environment for planting wishes, almost like a proverbial wishing well. Hypnosis may, on the surface, appear to be largely divorced from ancient healing practices, such as the Egyptian sleeping temples (see page 43), Shamanic ceremonies and yoga practices, but it shares a common root. While in a relaxed state, everyone is more suggestible. Relaxed states, such as those experienced during meditation, daydreams, deep relaxation, prayer or savasana at the end of yoga, allow us to access the hypnagogic state, a phase between waking and sleeping, when our conscious or critical minds are more relaxed.

Contrary to popular misconception, hypnosis, including self-hypnosis, is not about being 'put to sleep' and being made to do something you have no control over. In fact, you can't really do anything in hypnosis unless you want to do it. Trance states and hypnosis pervade our daily culture on many levels. They are used in advertising and social media, and when we watch a movie: we shrink our attention, allowing the content to sink into our subconscious awareness. When we are entranced in this way, our attention spirals into a state of narrow focus. When we are in this state, our subconscious minds become absorbed and our conscious minds relax. Everyone is more suggestible in this state. Remember: we are being conditioned all the time, and

have been since birth. In fact, we spend the first seven years of our lives in a sponge-like state of suggestibility, being conditioned by our environment, our relationships, our desires and other people's emotions and beliefs.

So, shouldn't we use this very trait as a tool to work for ourselves, as opposed to something that is hijacked? If other people are profiting (literally) from our state of suggestibility, why then can we not make use of it for the greater good of ourselves, our loved ones and our world? In this state, our imaginations are open and can be made available to work with us to imagine possibilities, positive futures and our wildest dreams. Creating a wishing state of mind might not be witchcraft, but it is a sort of magic!

THE WISHING MIND

When you are in a state of light relaxation or intentional hypnotic journeying, your mind becomes like a sacred well: a well of infinite imagination and spirit. This well provides an opportunity to cultivate a loving intimacy with yourself in a way that supports collaboration with your mind. When you think about how, on a certain level, our worries, phobias and fears are rooted in our imaginations running wild, you will see the clear advantages of learning to cultivate a wishing mind and knowing how to work with it. This will allow for a deep and compassionate intimacy with your imagination as you build a constellation of supportive internal references for who you are, and who you are becoming, and what you desire for your life.

MANIFESTATION: YOUR IMAGINATION IS A SUPER POWER

When you learn to coax your imagination into working for you, you'll soon find that it is, in fact, a hidden superpower that enables you to make your dreams come true. The idea that thoughts are causative is nothing new: mystics, kings and queens, philosophers and New Thought leaders have long believed in the power of imagination to affect thoughts and cause physical reactions in the body and material effects in the world. In fact, imagining and envisioning yourself succeeding is one of the primary elements of sports psychology, based on the scientific evidence that, when you imagine something in your mind, the brain processes it as if it's really happening. The Olympic athlete has the gold medal (in their mind) before they win the game. This doesn't mean they lie in bed all day dreaming about it: it means they use their imagination as a tool to motivate them into action.

You can try this yourself right now: imagine someone you love experiencing their greatest wish come true, and feel your heart expand and your lips turn up in a smile. Imagine your own greatest wish coming true, and feel energy rise up in your belly. Imagine biting into a juicy, ripe lemon, and feel your mouth begin to pucker and water. You see, the mind and body don't actually know the difference. This means that, by consciously imagining more of what we want, we can influence our energy to attract it; we can train our minds to see it, feel it and receive it.

The imagination is filled with thoughts and ideas that come together to create sensations in the body, influencing our emotions and behaviour. In other words, thoughts or ideas always precede creation: you think about what you want to eat, then you make it and you eat it. Once you get your own unique combination of thoughts, desires and sensations moving into action and towards the direction of your dreams, you will feel a gravitational pull that moves quickly, like a slipstream in a river, or a red carpet of motivation. Your imagination is an energetic or magnetic blueprint for attracting what you do – or do not – want in your life.

Each of us is said to have 60,000 thoughts a day – although I would imagine those numbers are increasing as our minds adapt and evolve due to the pervasive influence of social media and its incessant onslaught of images, advertising and information. Whatever the number, those thoughts don't necessarily matter unless we make them matter by giving them our attention.

Manifestation is popularly understood in terms of the Law of Attraction, which begins with the premise that like attracts like or thoughts become things. This refers to theories derived from quantum physics that posit how everything in the Universe has a vibration, including our thoughts, which respond to energy around them by resonating at the same frequency. In other words, we can use the energy of our thoughts to attract the energy that we want. This means that we attract into our lives what we think, believe and imagine most vividly.

I repeat: the mind and body don't know the difference between what's real or imagined; this means that we can imagine more of what we want consciously and we can influence our energy to attract it, train our mind to see it, feel it and receive it. We can also increase our conscious awareness of the imaginary things we don't want more of (like worry and anxiety) and we can work to shift and heal those unconscious patterns of influence and updating our awareness with a more positive supportive default mode.

This can carry with it a certain amount of anxiety: what if your thoughts are negative? After all, unconscious

thoughts and beliefs can influence us and attract things into our life that we don't necessarily want.

WishCraft suggests, however, that you don't have to believe everything you think – and you certainly don't have to feel shame or fear around your thoughts. In fact, when practising WishCraft, we can increase our conscious awareness of the thoughts and things we don't want more of, like worry and anxiety, and we can work to shift and heal those influential unconscious patterns. We can work to expand our capacity to have compassion for ourselves and others so that we can do the deeper healing necessary to move beyond debilitating shame and unconscious blocks. We can use our imaginations to influence and craft thoughts and words into magic wands to work with us instead of against us.

Thoughts are powerful tools in the art of manifesting, but we shouldn't be afraid of them. We can easily change them: your imagination is the real superpower. This means that when we work with our imagination, we begin to collaborate with our wishing, and this causes us to influence ourselves more supportively and deeply. In fact, this is the point of cultivating a supportive relationship with your creative mind.

Of course, although thoughts always precede creation (you think about what you want to eat and then you eat it), these magnetic blueprints for rapidly changing your life should not be misunderstood. Unlike popular understandings of the Law of Attraction, just because you think a bad thought doesn't automatically mean that bad things happening are your fault.

Personally, I find this idea to be harmful and victim blaming. For example, if a person has really low self-esteem and they are told, 'you make your own reality, so just start thinking differently', the Law of Attraction can backfire, causing them to further blame themselves. This can be damaging, and cause toxic shame which in turn defeats the wishing mind's generative, compassionate, abundance mindset.

Learning to use your wishing mind to increase the awareness of the words you use, and to disrupt the repeating repeating narratives and limiting beliefs of your inner dialogue is what helps you realise that yes, thoughts are just things, and you are not your thoughts. With the right words, wishing and will, you can change your mind and change your life.

CHANGEWORK: LIFE AS A COSMIC SPIRAL

Ultimately the difference between wishful thinking and WishCraft is what I call 'changework'. This means using the energy of our imagination and our wishes to literally change our minds, thus bringing our intentions into action. When considering how to make your wishes come true and how change works, it is important to remember we don't have to believe everything we think, and that we can choose which thoughts to focus on. In fact, we can actually change our minds by changing our thoughts. Studies on neuroplasticity suggest that changing your thought patterns through repetition – for example, by regularly repeating affirmations with strong emotional associations, or regular wishing rituals – can create new neural pathways in the brain. As these neural pathways grow and strengthen, they can help to change the way we think.

But this doesn't happen in a straightforward way. Our brains are sometimes refered to as being like computers— the implication being we can 'reprogramme' them at will. But I like to think of our mind as being more like a mushroom. That is, a natural, organic organism that works with external stiumli in its own magical way. In fact, it happens in a non-linear way; the brain scans of neural pathways are remarkably similar to photos of mushrooms growing. Just as mushrooms grow in a non-linear way under the soil, connecting resources from one tree to another (the reason that mushrooms are often referred to as the internet of the forest), our thoughts can change positively when we learn to use our imagination to help connect them to other positive thoughts in a non-linear collaborative way. Rather than growth happening in a straight line, when we engage with changework, life becomes a spiral, moving ever forwards, and sideways, and upwards, as our awareness of the world expands.

Over the years, I have had the exquisite honour of acting as a midwife to the dreams of many a wishing mind, and from many different vantage points: on the side of a cliff overlooking the Adriatic Sea on a Croatian island; in hospitals at the bedsides of people in recovery from various illnesses; at the wedding of my sister as she married the love of her life. I've shared and witnessed the beauty of people believing in their wishes and the possibility of change, even if only for a moment. I have seen people put their doubts aside and come to believe in themselves. And that is truly a sight to behold: to witness the undoing of the cultural and social conditioning that tells us we are not good enough, or not modest enough to take a risk in the direction of our dreams; to see the idea that we should only do something for the sake of winning, or to achieve a particular outcome, fall away and to be replaced with the wish to do and be well, no matter what.

And wishing well for oneself is often no easy feat, whether only for a minute or for a lifetime of practice. There are very real socio-economical, racial and wealth divides, privileges, traumas and other factors contributing to a person's belief in their ability to manifest positive change in their life. Not to mention there is a very real negativity bias that the brain has developed as an evolutionary response to protect us. This means that negativity and trauma register with more gravity than positivity and progress.

WishCraft is a system of wishing and self-hypnosis designed to counterbalance this. Rather than deny or bypass the difficulties in our lives, it is my attempt to provide practical tools and rituals to help reclaim the power of your imagination; to help find space to dream in the present moment; to bring non-judgement and compassion to the feelings of shame

that often prevent us from reaching our dreams; and to help find possibility and create a more fertile ground for hope, enabling us to move forward positively in our own way and in our own time, just as mushrooms grow in a non-linear lateral way.

A few years ago I was on a WishCraft tour offering my workshops and one-to-one ceremonies in various different countries. I remember a Sunday afternoon in London, I was looking out the window watching the rain and noticing the heaviness of the grey overcast skies as I was waiting for a client to arrive for a WishCraft ceremony. When she walked in the door, her expression and posture seemed to match the melancholy feeling outside the window, I could tell she wasn't feeling that well, in fact it wasn't long into the session that she began to cry and tell me of her recent struggles. She had been suffering from terrible stomach infections that she had contracted while travelling, and after months of trying to recover using various treatments and remedies, she was serious unwell, her health steadily deteriorating. Having been experiencing stress, anxiety, low energy and debilitating pain, she remarked how during the hypnosis she was able to deeply relax. So much so that she was able to imagine manifesting health, vitality and energy. She felt that this allowed for a healing process to occur while in the grips of her illness.

She was able to experience her future healed self now, and it gave her a real sense of hope and possibility that her situation could change for the better in a very real and tangible way, something she had not been able to create space to be able to imagine and create before.

What changed for her was that she was able to imagine her future self being out of pain, wearing her bright yellow jacket and having the energy to walk to a shop. Even though it felt unrealistic at the time, during the WishCraft session the experience felt so real, she saw and felt herself healed and was walking around as that healed version of herself - it opened up a whole new timeline of possibility. After several sessions she walked into a shop wearing her bright yellow jacket smiling and thought to herself, here I am, living as the future self I envisioned. Within just a few months was feeling so much stronger, healthier and clearer.

The hope she gained from that experience became an anchor for her ongoing healing. It helped her to continue to imagine herself well. She could work towards that positive outcome, even if it just meant revisiting that same vision over and over again. I learnt for her when in a deeply relaxed state the body and mind come into harmony and automatically lean towards the trajectory of healing.

WishCraft helped her believe that healing was possible and opened her to the positive everyday experiences and manifestations that she felt seriously sped up my healing process and showed her that she had a lot of the inner resources she could ever need inside her already.

On another occasion the WishCraft results came through more like a prophetic vision. In the part of our session where we were role playing the future as if it had already happened, a client began to get really creative and hopeful. When I asked about her favourite thing that had happened 'last year' she remarked: "Oh, it was meeting the love of my life!" I, very excited for this imagined future, inquired further: "How wonderful! Where did you meet them?" Without hesitation, she replied: "outside my building. He is wearing a blue suit and he works nearby. I feel so adored and safe when I'm around him." Lo and behold, a few months later, she returns for a session only to tell me that she had fallen in love, with man she met standing outside her building, wearing a blue suit. Fast forward seven years later, and I always smile when I receive a holiday card with a photo of her and family. She told me she still remembers the moment in our session when she allowed herself to believe that love was possible for her, how it felt like a big burst of joy, as if 'a firecracker of celebration and possibilities went off in my heart,' and that it was this that propelled her to believe it to be true when she met her future partner.

When we surrender to the moment and allow ourselves to feel deserving of good things happening to us and to those around us, we not only flood our minds and bodies with happy hormones and chemicals like dopamine and serotonin, we also signal to our bodies that we are there for ourselves in the same way that we would be for a loved one or a friend. We begin to establish an intimate, well-wishing rapport with our innermost selves.

To make this process really easy and repeatable I've created an acronym to guide you in your own changework practice. Overleaf, I have given an example of own of my own past wishes, to help explain the acronym.

W.I.S.H.

Healing and change

What do you wish for? Write down your intention.

I wished to be more confident and take risks to travel and try new things.

Identify the resistance and integrate it with healing thoughts and feelings using your imagination.

I identified my insecurities were coming from my scared inner child, who felt insecure and alone.

Soften into the resistance with compassion. Befriend and collaborate with the parts of you that need healing or encouragement.

I imagined my adult self comforting my little self with love and tenderness.

Harmonise and heal the resource into the resistance. Imagine yourself healing and responding differently to the old resistance or limiting belief.

I integrated the scared little child with resources from my adult self, established a supportive loving relationship between these two parts of me so that healing could easily flow back and forth.

C.R.A.F.T.

Change and transformation

C ollaborate with yourself with compassion.

I allowed myself to take a chance to travel and move abroad. Even if insecurity came up, my scared inner child was no longer in control. I was able to anchor into courage and take a chance despite feeling fear.

R eframe the problem with new possibilities and perspectives.

I thought of the best possibilities and I got excited about them. If I felt insecurity I felt compassion for myself instead of shame and I allowed myself to make mistakes and have fun.

A ffirm it with your words and mental images, take Action in the direction of your dreams.

I enjoyed dreaming and imagining all the good things, I let it motivate me without attachments to the outcome.

F eel it as if it already is.

I amplified these good feelings and associations when I was exercising, when I was dancing, when I was daydreaming, until I felt like confidently travelling the world was already a part of my life.

T ransform positively and patiently.

By taking more chances I began to co-create a life I loved. I found myself in real-life situations that were even greater than I could have imagined.

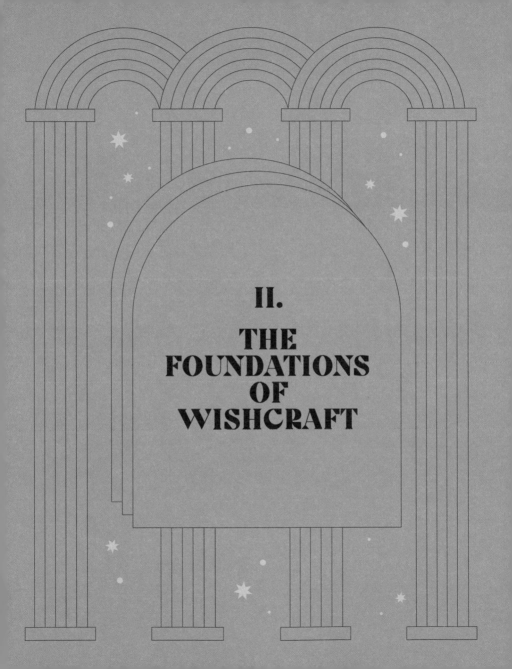

II.

THE
FOUNDATIONS
OF
WISHCRAFT

HISTORY, SYMBOLS & MYTHOLOGY TO INSPIRE YOUR WISHING

HISTORY OF HYPNOSIS: THE MEDICINE OF THE IMAGINATION

Throughout the ages, the practice of wishing has been, in essence, about transformation. True transformation takes time and courage: bravery is needed to enter into the unknown. True transformation is having the strength to go your own way. True transformation takes determination: you must be willing to go deep within yourself in order to reclaim the sovereignty of your imagination, the part of you which is not influenced by your parents, education or society.

Hypnosis is one of the easiest, oldest and most misunderstood tools for transformation. Although, the trance state that is accessed in hypnosis is often compared to meditation, not only is it a state of relaxation, but it is also an ideal state in which to transform thoughts, beliefs, and behaviours (what I have just introduced you to as changework, see pages 31–35).

The earliest recorded example of hypnosis or suggestion therapy dates back to Ancient Egypt, where people would make pilgrimages to the 'sleeping temples' – now thought of as the original hospitals – in order to seek healing for all sorts of ailments. In these temples, they would be induced into a trance-like state by the priestess or priest through the use of drumming and chanting. In this trance state, the patients would connect to their local deity and a sort of 'psychic surgery' was performed through the use of 'suggestion therapy' or hypnosis. Allegedly these surgeries would result in miraculous healing. It was presumably a powerful mix of ritual, expectation and suggestion and can be understood in modern times in terms of the placebo effect – a term that refers to the combinartion of ritual, expectation, and context that all play a role in one's healing. In other words when one believes they have been cured, measurable physiological and psychological changes produce healing results.

In the late eighteenth and early nineteenth centuries, German doctor Franz Anton Mesmer (from whose name the word 'mesmerised' is derived) popularised an early version of hypnosis, which was referred to as animal magnetism. This 'magnetism' was said to activate a sort of 'magnetic fluid' or 'life-force energy' within his patients that would cause spontaneous healing. His approach was later discredited on the basis that it was nothing more than 'the medicine of the imagination'. Upon uncovering this phrase in the history books, it struck me that this was, in fact, an accurate and empowering definition of hypnosis. By extension, I like to refer to WishCraft as 'the medicine of the imagination'.

If we accept the power of surrendering our desires and worries to a (perceived) force that is greater than us (or our conscious awareness), we find that we are capable of more than the conscious mind can conceive. This, in essence, is the power of belief. Just as the Celtic people surrendered their wishes to the gods living in the wishing wells, and just as people surrender their prayers to a higher power, in the case of WishCraft, we surrender to the imagination as a field of possibility or a force of infinite potential. This is what I mean when I refer to the beneficial act of 'surrendering to the supportive forces within us and around us'. It is part of the process of making your dreams come true.

It is the wishing well.

The idea of the wishing well has its origins in European folklore and the ancient Celtic tradition. In ancient Celtic culture, water was regarded as sacred, and not only for its practical, life-giving qualities of cleansing and nourishment; many believed it had magical properties and was the dwelling place of the gods. A wishing well could be found at the centre of many towns and was seen as a place of hope: when people went to the well, they would surrender their wishes and worries to the gods. In my workshops, I often joke that the wishing well was the original therapist.

Although the notion of gods dwelling in the water is no longer commonplace, people continue to visit wishing wells. It's reported that wishing wells around the world make millions every year: in fact, the Trevi Fountain in Rome is estimated to collect 3,000 euros ($3,500) a day in coins from wishes. This is a testament to how present and pervasive the practice of wishing is in our everyday lives.

If WishCraft had an official element, it would be water. Throughout history, and in many cultures, water has been, and continues to be, regarded with reverence. From the waters of baptism to the holy healing water of Lourdes, France, and the sacred pilgrimages made to the Ganges in India, water is an enduring symbol of hope and redemption and an ideal element for wishing.

In Chinese philosophy, water is highly regarded, respected for its life-sustaining powers and its ability to take on whatever shape holds it. There is an old zen proverb that states 'the wise adopt themselves to circumstances as water molds itself to the tea pot.' The suggestion being that water reflects and adapts to the shape of its surroundings.

Considering the properties of water, symbolically and metaphorically, will enrich and deepen your wishing journey. Water quite literally surrounds us: it covers seventy-one per cent of the Earth and composes sixty-five per cent of our bodies. What better way to symbolically surrender to the supportive forces within us and around us, than by looking to the qualities of water to guide us on how to live our lives and how to make our wishes flow into reality? It's no wonder our ancestors have been wishing on it for thousands of years.

ST BRIGID: GODDESS OF WISHES

In Irish culture, St Brigid, who has the notable status of being both a goddess and a saint, is known in the pagan tradition as the goddess of the sacred well, fire and healing, and in the Catholic tradition as the patron saint of poetry, fugitives and sailors. She represents the pagan holiday of Imbolc, celebrating the mid-point between the winter solstice and the spring equinox, and acts as a custodian or intermediary between the darkness and the light; the seeds below the earth in winter and the flowers blooming in spring; the conscious and the subconscious. If there were a patron saint of WishCraft, it would be Brigid. On our wishing journeys, we can learn from her wisdom and look to both darkness and light as we follow our dreams into action. Cultivating a self-hypnosis and WishCraft practice creates space in our mind to embrace both the dark and the light, creating an integrative mindscape. Brigid can inspire us to have courage in our changework and just as she transforms seeds to flowers, winter to spring, or darkness to light, we are reminded to bring patience and nourishment to the shadowy parts of ourselves that need healing and compassion on our wishing journey, trusting in our nature to change and grow.

Why consider the history of wishing? I am writing this book from my home in New York City in the year 2020. A time of rapid change, it seems that that every day brings something unexpected, politically, environmentally and socially, and not only in the world, but to each of us as individuals. This level of global uncertainty has never been experienced in my lifetime, and in these challenging times, I find comfort and wisdom in learning about the history and traditions of wishing, and in particular looking to characteristics of water for guidance. In life, and in the manifestation process, water and wishing can remind us to surrender and go with the flow, to give ourselves to others without expecting anything in return, to be flexible and to be free. After all, we are all descended from ancestors who endured great hardship and yet yielded continual progress: perhaps our human ability to wish and hope for positive outcomes is part of what helped them overcome, innovate and evolve.

WISHING TRADITIONS FROM DIFFERENT CULTURES

True transformation takes place when you realise that, at the core of your being, you are a wishing well of possibilities. As we have been exploring in this chapter, the varying traditions of wishing have given humans moments of freedom in which we can choose hope over fear and the future over the past. Wishing helps us to move beyond our limitations and labels; it opens us up to different energies and perspectives, enabling us to see beyond what our conscious minds can conceive. It encourages us to engage with a whole world of possibility within us and around us.

Water and wells are not the only things associated with wishing, far from it. Following are some of my favourite popular wishing traditions or rituals. Whether you find them silly, superstitious or super fun, they are all part of long-held traditions with practical, folkloric roots that have helped humans harness their attention as a way of manifesting hope and achieving transformation. After each explanation are suggestions for how to incorporate these into updated wishing rituals.

Ancient Greeks and Artemis, goddess of hunting and the Moon, are probably to thank for the beloved tradition of blowing out candles on birthday cakes. It is said that cakes and other treats were brought to the temple of Artemis as offerings and were adorned with candles to emulate the glow of the moon. It was believed that the smoke from the candles brought messages or prayers to the gods. The superstition, even now, is to blow out the candles on a cake and make a silent wish.

***

When wishing on a birthday candle, take a moment to stare into the flame. Think of what you wish for yourself. Imagine yourself receiving it. Breathe into your heart, count to three and blow out your wish.

Wishing on eyelashes was common in mid-nineteenth century England. The practice generally involved the wisher placing a fallen eyelash on the back of their hand before throwing it over their shoulder. If the eyelash got stuck, the wish would not come true. Another version, said to have been popular among young girls in Cornwall, called for the eyelash to be placed on the tip of the wisher's nose; if she managed to blow it off, she'd get her wish.

***

If you are lucky enough to catch a fallen eyelash on your face or a friend's, seize this moment of intersecting chance and destiny and blow your eyelash into the air, imagining the wish that you wish coming true.

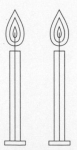

STARS

The idea of wishing on stars can be linked back to the ancient Latin word *'desiderare'*, meaning to long for or to wish for something. This word may come from *'de sidere'* – 'from the stars'. It is a tradition that is still well-known today – many of us grew up with the familiar rhyme:

Starlight, star bright,
The first star I see tonight,
I wish I may, I wish I might,
Have the wish I wish tonight.

Ptolemy, a Greco-Egyptian writer, mathematician and astronomer, believed that shooting stars were a sign that the gods were looking down and listening to wishes. Sort of puts a more intimate spin on the experience of the infinite night sky, if you ask me.

***

Tonight, or any night where you find yourself gazing up at the night sky, close your eyes for a moment and, upon opening them, make a wish on the first or brightest star you see. Focus in on its light. Imagine this light is as old as the Universe itself and remember that we are made of stardust. Stand there for a moment, soaking that starlight into your wish. Wish your wish, and imagine it coming true.

LADYBIRDS

These cute little insects are said to get their name from the Virgin Mary, often called 'Our Lady'. The red of the beetle echoes the red cloak in which Mary was often depicted in Medieval times, while the black spots are said to represent her sorrows. The bugs have long been thought of as a good omen for farmers, due to their appetite for eating harmful pests and so protecting crops. Farmers would often pray to the Virgin Mary to protect their crops, and if ladybirds showed up, their crops would be saved.

Because of this, ladybirds are considered good luck; if one lands on you, it is believed to grant you a wish.

***

Next time you find a ladybird making its way across your body, consider yourself lucky and imagine a little blessed insect genie is there for you, ready to grant your wish. Make your wish and thank the ladybird for making it come true.

Numerologists and mystics suggest that the symmetry of repeating numbers such as 11:11 are symbols of an auspicious synchronicity. Seeing these numbers is supposed to signal a sort of message from the Universe that you are on the right path: perhaps guardian angels are speaking to you through these number alignments (like a window from the spirit world), thus making it an ideal time for manifestations and wishes, knowing the spirits are right there by your side (or in your clock).

***

When you find yourself in the same moment as these repeating numbers, imagine you just got caught in a cosmic elevator with your guardian angels or well-wishing faeries. Ask for support in your wishes coming true or trust in higher guidance and support in manifesting your wishes.

Commonly seen as symbols of love and union, dandelions were popular wishing tools in nineteenth-century Europe, allegedly providing insight into one's romantic life – which explains the famous 'He loves me, he loves me not' chant that is repeated while plucking dandelion leaves. Dreams about dandelions were said to refer to love and marriage, and it was also commonly believed that, if you blew on a dandelion and all the seeds flew away, your loved one returned your feelings; but if any seeds remained, they might have reservations, or no feelings for you at all. Dandelion tea was also purported to increase psychic abilities. Wishing on a dandelion in a flower-filled field on a sunny day has just the amount of drama I like in my wishing, and it's no coincidence that a conceptual dandelion graces the cover of this book.

***

When you find yourself in a field of dandelions gone to seed, take a moment to choose the fluffiest one. Hold the fullest part of the dandelion close your mouth, being careful to point in the direction of the wind. Take a deep breath in, imagining your wish. Blow the seeds into the wind and watch your wishes take flight.

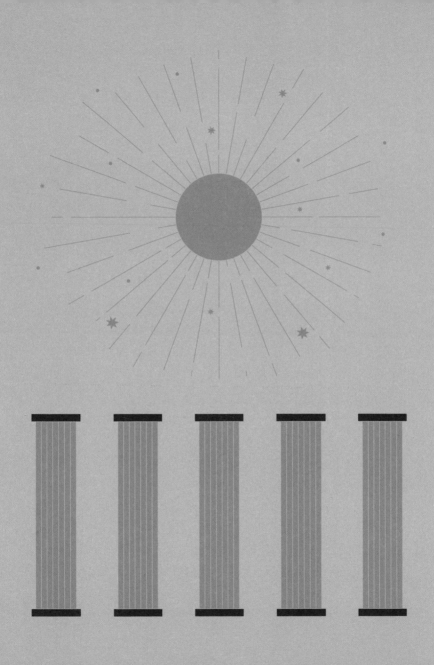

THE PILLARS OF WISHCRAFT

The idea of WishCraft is supported by five key pillars: self- collaboration, compassion, creativity, curiosity and community. Without them, you cannot effectively practise WishCraft. With them, and by learning to implement them consistently and in your own way, you can learn how to make your wishes come true, as you train your brain to become more receptive to abundance and positivity.

Self-appreciation + self-intimacy = self-collaboration

Learn to thank yourself. By doing so, you cultivate a mindset of appreciation for yourself. Thank yourself for being you; for the things you do for yourself and for other people; for the things you've overcome; for the things you've tried but didn't succeed at; for the things you love and like about yourself.

Get into the practice of thanking yourself as if you're your own best friend. Cultivate this habit on a daily basis. An ideal time to do it is just before bed, at a time when we are slipping into the liminal state between waking and sleeping and we are more receptive to suggestion. I recommend choosing three moments from your day that you can thank yourself for. Look back and review your three moments. Repeat these thanks to yourself: repetition makes us more receptive to suggestion. I suggest using your name to create a sense of intimacy and friendship with yourself. The mind makes new patterns and pathways through repetition and reinforcement – it's just like building and toning muscle. The better we get at believing in ourselves in an unconditional way, at wanting the best for ourselves and at wishing ourselves well regardless of the outcome, the more we will be able to take positive actions in the direction of our dreams. We will be building on this practice later in the book.

Love + kindness = compassion

Spend time in self-hypnosis, using a trance-like, meditative state to help you connect to those people who you love and appreciate. Connect that compassion to the parts of you that struggle, feel blocked or are in pain. Connect to the future you, for whom your wishes have already come true.

You can do this by setting aside a time to journey inside yourself. Listen to a guided meditation or ambient music and set your intention to explore meeting with these different parts of yourself with compassion. You may not actually achieve these meetings: your mind may wander and doubt, which is totally normal. The main thing is that you dedicate time and intention to this. It's an exercise in mind training.

Imagination + action = creativity

Make a plan of action. Break down your wishes into smaller wishes: weekly, monthly, seasonally. Connect and commit to other people and places to bring your wishes into action. Take your wishes from fantasy into imagination: your imagination is a place where you can be actively creative and begin to explore how you will take action. It's not about if your wish happens, it's about how. With this mindset, we can train the brain to become better at finding solutions, better at recognising what we are looking for – and better at receiving it!

Attention + interest = curiosity

Curiosity is when we learn to cultivate our attention and become interested in the present moment. When we allow ourselves to be curious we see things differently. The experience of wishing vs. the experience of having are often quite different. The wishing can become a high that feels almost better than the real thing. When we get too attached to wishing, the having itself can feel disappointing or difficult because it involves being present with uncertainty. Learning to be curious teaches us to get comfortable with the element of surprise and to appreciate what we have, it builds a mindset of resilience and receptivity. This balance of wishing and becoming curious and comfortable with uncertainty builds a sustainable environment for our wishing in which it becomes much easier to 'surrender to the supportive forces within us' as our wishes come true. Curiosity is a skill we can develop and can be practised everyday, using our powers of observation and attention more fully. We become more sensitive to what is happening now, noticing what is, not what we wanted or expected it to be. We begin to enjoy the pleasures of surprise and uncertainty. Practise this by reminding yourself of the ways in which you have been pleasantly surprised by thinking back to five positive events in your life that began with an uncertain, unknown outcome and ended up positive. Think of live events, challenges you've overcome, unlikely accomplishments and relationships that turned out well. The odds are you will find surprise plays a significant role in your joyful experiences as well as on your wishing journey.

Commitment + collaboration = community

Commit to sharing and collaborating with your community. I once had a psychotherapist who told me: 'There is no happiness without commitment.' That has stayed with me throughout the years, inspiring me to commit to my dreams and finding that this does indeed bring happiness. Community encourages accountability and accountability fosters commitments. Share your gifts and talents and time, reach out to people you admire and offer your time or words of gratitude. Create a community or circle of WishCrafters to be accountable to and with whom you can foster mutual support and appreciation.

Understand that we are all interconnected: the air we breathe, the water we drink and the stars we wish on are all made of the same material. We are all interdependent. Alone we go fast, together we go far.

SELF-COLLABORATION

COMPASSION

CREATIVITY

CURIOSITY

COMMUNITY

SIMPLE STEPS TO FINDING YOUR WISHING MIND

Your wishing mind is how you bring your wish (or intention) into alignment with your energy (or your body), a way to move the wish out of your head and into your emotions and imagination and then into action. Below are the steps to drop into your wishing mind. Pick a serene, soothing space where you can light candles and listen to ambient music (music without words tends to create a blank space for your mind to wander and wish free of emotional associations or anchors). I suggest somewhere where you can lie down comfortably: maybe your sofa, or even the floor. You can use your bed, but make it feel special and different to how it is when you go to bed to sleep.

1. Write down your wish. You could start with wishing for something very simple for yourself to start with. This could be anything from wishing for a sunny day to wishing to spend an afternoon with a good friend in the park.

2. Take three deep breaths. Imagine breathing in the energy of 'gratitude', and breathing out the energy of 'love'. As you do this, imagine dropping your mind into your body, settling into one space.

3. Now, think of your wish, and imagine where the energy of your wish is in your body. It could be in your heart, your stomach – anywhere.

4. Breathe in again, thinking of your wish. Engage with that wish. If your wish was a colour, what colour would it be? If your wish was an emotion, what emotion would it be?

5. Continue breathing and giving life to your wish.

6. Place your hand on the part of your body where you have imagined the wish being. Continue to breathe.

7. Now, focus on the energy of your wish moving around your body, stemming from its original place. This is your wishing mind; it is working for you and not against you. It's a sacred well of intentional energy, a reservoir of unlimited resources always available to you.

8. Repeat step 2, breathing in and out three times, breathing in gratitude and breathing out love, then slowly come back into the room.

III.

WAYS
TO
WISH

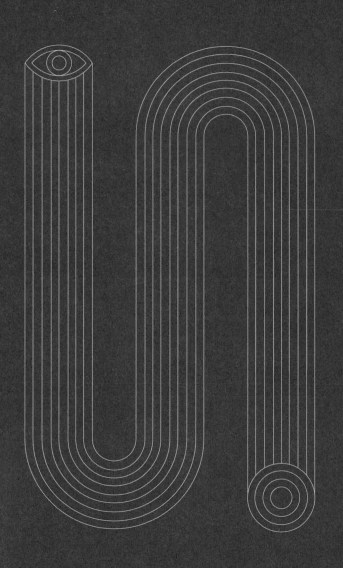

THE
OVERVIEW
EFFECT

*'Life is based on perception. Perception is based
on opinion. Opinion is based on thought.
Thought comes from the mind. Change your mind.
Change your world.'*

– ANONYMOUS

When astronauts look down on Earth from outer space,
they may experience a cognitive shift in awareness known
as the overview effect. Astronauts who have experienced
this have reported feeling suddenly aware of and awestruck
by how small and fragile the Earth seems in the vastness
of the Universe, an overwhelming feeling that is hard to
comprehend unless you, too, have seen it in this way.

By using our imaginations, and through the practice
of self-hypnosis, we can achieve something similar. We can
have an overview experience of our own lives by viewing them
from a place of awe and appreciation for who we are, and
who we are becoming. Remember: WishCraft is a practice and
process, and it takes time. Practise patience in your wishing,
and allow yourself to be where you are. Be gentle with
yourself: wish and work with your wishes in your own time
and in your own way. Healing and receiving take time and
often don't follow a direct line.

CULTIVATING YOUR PRACTICE

In WishCraft, just as in life, patience is a virtue. By that, I mean your wishes may take time to come to fruition. Learning to enjoy the *process* as you *progress*, is the best approach to making your wishes come true. I like to think of the mind as a garden and wishes as the seeds you plant. Learning to cultivate your wishing practice will help you grow flowers, not weeds.

In this section, I'm going to explain ways to wish well for yourself, other people and the world. When I say 'wish well', I am talking about wishing with kindness and care for yourself and others.

The ways to wish we will explore in this chapter are foundational self-hypnosis exercises that will help to increase your self-worth, clear blocks and empower your spirit with an attitude of appreciation and energetic magnetism. These exercises will also bring up a lot of feelings, and that is a good thing: it means that energy is moving. Allow your feelings to flow – the joy, the sadness – without thinking or judging.

Once you have become familiar with the methods and practices in this chapter, you can use them as ways of wishing. In chapter four, you'll find suggested wording for some of the most common wishes, for things like love, success and forgiveness. You can use this wording in some of the exercises and rituals here, or create your own.

There is no right or wrong way to experience your wishing mind. You may see things, you may feel things, you may hear things or just get a sense of them. Given that the substance of WishCraft is your imagination, remember this is a creative process, and thus you can expect a healthy amount of trial and error. When developing the wishing state of mind, not only are you going to learn to manifest your wishes into reality, you're going to build a more supportive relationship with yourself. When we wish, we may experience negative, critical self-talk and doubt, especially at first. This is normal and is thanks in part to the brain's negativity bias. That's why you tend to ruminate over the one bad thing your friend said to you, as opposed to all the good things that they also said. However, as we begin to better understand our practice, we know that (thanks to neuroplasticity) we can focus on strengthening new, positive neural pathways and associations, just like when we exercise muscles. Over time, these exercises will train your mind to become better and better at believing in yourself.

The most important thing is to have fun with it! In Hindu mythology, it is said that the Brahman created the world in the highest state of consciousness, or *'Lila'*, which translates as a state of play. Play and playfulness are the magic sauce of manifestation. To paraphrase one of my favourite writers, Oscar Wilde: 'Life is too important to be taken seriously.' When you get the hang of ways to wish well, it becomes seriously fun!

Wishing for oneself is where it all starts. It can be a bit awkward at first, as we are not used to, and often not encouraged to, wish well for ourselves. It can be seen as selfish or self-centred, an idea that can be intensified by the negativity bias explained on page 68. However, in my practice, and over years of perfecting the art of WishCraft, I've found the daily habit of self-appreciation and wishing well for myself to be the single most powerful tool for healing my insecurities and increasing my self-worth. Ultimately, it has allowed for a spirit of greater generosity and sincerity for supporting the wishes of others and the world.

①

Begin by writing down ten qualities or characteristics that you love and appreciate about yourself. If it helps, think of compliments that other people have given you for inspiration. For example, I love that I'm adventurous, I love my love of dancing, I love my ability to forgive, etc. Jot them down. Don't worry about your penmanship or getting the most elegant wording – the important thing is to get them on paper. The reason for writing this list down longhand is that scientific studies suggest this makes it more likely to encode in your long-term memory, and we want this to stick.

 ②

After writing down your list of things you love about yourself, read it aloud to yourself, ideally while looking into a mirror (when starting out, you don't have to stand too close). Alternatively, you can record yourself reading the list aloud (try not to be critical of how you look or the sound of your own voice in the recording). If you find it too weird to read this list aloud at first, take the time to read it to yourself in your mind and let it sink in a bit.

After you write and repeat these things that you love about yourself, you will feel almost 100 per cent better than you did when you started. This is, in part, thanks to your neurons firing off happy hormones and chemicals like dopamine and serotonin. This positive, abundant state of mind is the antidote to the anxious 'fight or flight' state of mind that is ruled by negativity bias. When you are in an abundance mindset, you will find yourself in a state of resourcefulness and appreciation, a state open to collaboration. By bringing your attention here, you are bringing your mind to a state of self-appreciation similar to a state of gratitude, except here it comes from the inside out and assumes your happiness is unconditional. You should aim to be in this state of appreciation, especially self-appreciation, whenever you want to manifest or make your wishes come true. This concept is often referred to in the Law of Attraction as 'Like attracts like'.

Now, take a moment and write down what you wish for yourself over the next six months or year, or whatever timeframe feels most natural to you. Think of ten things that you would really love to see happen for yourself in the near future. Remember to have fun with it – imagine the best year or six months ever!

Once you've completed your 'wish list', repeat the step above: read your wishes aloud to yourself in the mirror or record yourself saying them. If the wishes on your list align with any of the wishes in chapter four, you can use the wording given there. If not, you can come up with your own.

⑥

After you do this, I encourage you to time-travel in your imagination. Remember that, in your mind, it's all happening together – the past, the present and the future – and, with hypnosis, you can explore all parts and all phases of yourself and your life with new resources and perspectives. So, imagine that you have time-travelled into the future, to six months or one year from now, and all your wishes have come true. Role-play with yourself (again, in the mirror or recording yourself). Imagine that you are catching up with yourself one year from now. Ask yourself (and answer):

✳ What was your favourite thing that happened last year?

✳ What did you give to yourself to support that happening?

✳ What daily thought patterns and habits helped you to manifest your wishes?

✳ Did you have to let go of something in order to create more space for the wishes to come true?

Remember to speak in the past tense, because your wishes have already come true!

The main thing here is to have fun with it. It's not about whether it feels real or not, it's about playing with ideas and allowing yourself to feel deserving of the life you wish to create for yourself.

The purpose of these exercises is to side-step your conscious mind and step into the realm of your imaginative mind. By writing down what you love and appreciate about yourself, you bring your attention to feeling good and worthy. By speaking your wishes out loud, you declare it to the Universe (the Universe loves commitment), and your mind begins to organise your desire in the direction of your wishes coming true. Finally, when you talk about your wishes as if they have already come true, you bypass the conscious mind in the same way we do in a trance state. On some level, the body doesn't know the difference between what's real or what's imagined. The messages being received are that the wishes have already come true. It's like fertiliser for your belief system. And now the trick is to collaborate with your future self and with the energy of your wishes, to wish yourself well and to bring that energy to where you need it most.

This is how you wish well for yourself and work to manifest your wishes: you bring yourself to an 'overview place' of appreciation and abundance for yourself and your surroundings; you bring that energy into words and you cast a spell with your imagination, a proclamation and commitment that drive you forwards and help you to move through fear and into courage – into action.

The exercises here are meant to be an extension of the
fertile wishing ground that we have planted on pages 70–73
in 'Wishing for yourself'.

WISHING WELL FOR THE OTHER PARTS OF YOURSELF

One of my favourite techniques in self-hypnosis is using
parts therapy. Parts therapy (derived from Internal Family
Systems therapy) suggests that the self is made up of different
parts and, through using our imagination, we can build
relationships with the different parts of ourselves as a means
to integrate into a more harmonious whole self. In wishing
for others, we will first begin wishing for the other parts of
ourselves that need healing, integration and attention. As one
of my favourite hypnosis teachers, John Overdurf, says: 'No
matter what you think you are, you are always more than that.'

When thinking of wishing for the different parts of
yourself, imagine coming from a place of support for your
future self. You might even begin to construct a sort of 'super
wisher' or ultimate wish-giver inside of you: a kind of 'inner
wish genie' or 'Fairy Wish-mother'. To help you focus on this
idea, think of three qualities to give your inner wish genie
and write them down. You may even come up with an image
of what they look like, or give them a name.

Once you have established this perspective of power
and well-wishing, write down three wishes for each part
of you as listed overleaf. If the wishes you write down align
with any of the wishes in chapter four, you can use the
wording given there. If not, you can come up with your own.

①

Write three wishes for your 'little self', otherwise known as your inner child. Our past selves can receive our well wishes. Imagine your little self receiving them now: safe, secure and protected by your present self.

②

Write three wishes for your 'shadow self' or inner critic. Again, you may decide to give it a name and imagine what it looks like. This one can be tricky, as sometimes it isn't easy to wish well for our inner critic. The main thing here is to think in terms of healing and compassion. Remember that hurt people hurt people: the odds are that your inner critic is hurting below their criticism. Remember, too, that you can give yourself whatever it is that you and your inner critic really need. The inner critic may need a hug, or it may need a tough-love talking-to – do whatever feels best and most empowering to you. You can do a full healing ceremony with your inner critic, if you wish, or you can just begin the process.

③

Write three wishes for your present self. Imagine you are looking at your present self through the eyes of your future self: what does your future self appreciate about you and want for you?

'Just as I wish well for myself, may your wishes come true.' This incantation closes out almost every WishCraft ceremony I perform. Because in WishCraft, we realise that it's not me – it's *we*. Wishing well for others is sometimes easier than wishing well for ourselves. We are definitely more accustomed to and comfortable with directing our love and support towards others. Because love is the heart of courage (and fortune favours the brave, as they say), in the game of WishCraft the getting is in the giving, so to speak – but only when you do it for giving's sake. This next exercise is inspired by loving-kindness meditation, a Buddhist meditation that is based on compassion.

①

Think of someone you feel loved and supported by, and write down three things you love and appreciate about them. Now, in the wishing state of mind, try to imagine looking into their eyes and sharing with them what you love and appreciate about them. Imagine them receiving this love and appreciation. You might imagine light and energy flowing from your heart into theirs. Now imagine things from their perspective, through their eyes. Write down three things *they* love and appreciate about *you*. Feel them sending you that love and appreciation, and imagine yourself receiving it. Again, you might imagine light and energy flowing from their heart into yours.

②

Think of someone you admire and feel inspired by. Repeat the above process.

③

Finally, think of someone you feel jealous of, or sometimes feel resentment towards. Write down three ways in which you feel jealous of or threatened by them. Julia Cameron, author of *The Artist's Way,* refers to jealousy as a 'mask for fear' and suggests the antidote to that fear or jealousy is action. Think of the ways in which you feel jealous and imagine this jealousy instead as inspiration. Transform the three ways in which you feel jealous of them into three ways in which you feel inspired by them or what they are doing. Remind yourself of the three ways in which you love and appreciate yourself (from the list of things you love about yourself, page 78) and imagine a protective light and energy surrounding you. Let

this positive energy infuse that old toxic jealousy with creativity and appreciation for yourself, moving you into taking action towards your dreams and desires, fuelled by compassionate, unconditional well-wishing for yourself and others. Take a moment to feel happiness and support for the person you feel jealous of and imagine their wishes coming true, remembering the saying 'just as I wish well for myself, may your wishes come true'.

When wishing well for someone in the world that you don't know and will never meet, imagine someone your same age and who is struggling with the same things you are struggling with, but they don't have the resources that you have. Imagine sending them strength, gratitude or love. Imagine them receiving your wish for them to be well.

WISHING WELL FOR THE WORLD OR COMMUNITY

Wishing well for the world is understanding that our sense of self is inextricably entwined with all lives and living things. Think of the notion of 'oneness' that weaves through all spiritual schools of thought and consider the way that our identities expand beyond human relationships: that our beliefs, actions and breath interact with a shared world of which we are one part. Just as we breathe the oxygen created by plants many miles away, our thoughts and beliefs have an impact on our community and world. We can use these wishes as ways to connect us to the living system that is beyond ourselves, understanding that we all breathe the same air, drink the same water and wish on the same stars. These wishes are seeds for the collective manifestation of a better future.

① Think of a place in the world that you love: it can be a place to which you have a special connection, or a place that inspires you. Write down three wishes for that place, for its people, its animals and its land (all of them, or just ones you feel called to). If the wishes you write down align with any of the wishes in chapter four, you can use the wording given there. If not, you can come up with your own. In a wishing state of mind, imagine sending these wishes to this place. You might imagine yourself floating above the place and sending light and energy down into it, then imagine the place receiving that light and energy. Remember there is no right or wrong way to do this. Just use your imagination,

② Now think of a place that has given you support, nourishment or shelter. Write down three things that you appreciate about this place, or are grateful to it for. As before, write down three things that you wish for the place. Again, imagine it receiving those wishes and that appreciation, whether the people, the animals or the land.

③ Now think of a place in the world that needs help or could use more support. As above, write down three things you appreciate about it, and three things you wish for this place. Once again, imagine sending this place your well wishes, and imagine it receiving these wishes like light and energy.

④ As always, finish by repeating this incantation three times: 'Just as I wish well for myself, may your wishes come true.'

WISHING RITUALS

Ritual is an important element when it comes to focusing your attention and intention into the act of wishing. It infuses your wishes with blessings and significance. While all spiritual schools of thought and religions have their own ways of using rituals, the practice is more or less consistent. A ritual is something set apart from normal life and made special. You have already begun ritualising and bestowing your wishes with intention through the practice of cultivating your wishing mind. The following suggestions are ways to make your rituals more potent, powerful and pleasurable.

The famed artist Yoko Ono has an ongoing and very popular exhibit called *Wish Tree,* in which participants are invited to write down their wishes and tie them to trees. There is also an ancient practice that is still popular Ireland today, where people wrap strips of cloth around the trees near ancient holy wells as an offering or message to the spirit they are petitioning.

In my wishing ceremonies, I almost always have a conceptional wishing well. At one of my early WishCraft events, an artist had made a wishing well out of holographic paper and a neon hose which spouted coloured water. At the end of the ceremony, I gathered everyone around the wishing well to declare their wishes to the world, with one another as their witnesses. These days, I have one special wishing well (a white ceramic bowl etched with a floral pattern). It is very dear to my heart, and while not on duty at my wishing ceremonies, it holds court in the centre of my living room. On any given day, it is likely to be filled with silver tinsel, rose petals or written wishes, not only looking cute but also acting as a sacred container for my wishes coming true. In the case I don't have my wishing well with me for a ceremony, I will make one – and I always make sure it is special.

**INGREDIENTS FOR
RITUAL WISHING**

1. Candles, lighter or matches

2. Ambient or healing sounds or music without words

3. Flowers

4. Paper and pen

5. Notecards

6. Wishing bowl and water (remember the significance of water when it comes to wishing – see pages 45–46)

7. And, of course, don't forget to bring your wishing mind

Place some water in your wishing bowl. I like to bestow a prayer or blessing upon the water as it's being poured into the bowl. I usually do this by giving it thanks for its cleansing, healing and life-giving properties, as well as its ability to surrender to all that is around it.

Place flowers around the bowl (I prefer roses for their symbolism of endurance and beauty).

Make three wishes: one wish for yourself, one for someone you love and one for the world. If the wishes you choose align with any of the wishes in chapter four, you can use the wording given there. If not, you can come up with your own. Speak each wish out loud, slowly and affirmatively. Tear off a few rose petals as you state each wish and lovingly toss them into the water.

This is a favourite wishing ritual of mine. Take three tealight candles, and make a wish for your past, your present and your future. If the wishes you choose align with any of the wishes in chapter four, you can use the wording given there. If not, you can come up with your own. Write down each wish, then light each candle. Take time to stare into the flames, connecting to your wishing mind (perhaps by taking a few deep breaths, breathing in love and breathing out gratitude). State your wish for your past self aloud. Imagine your past self receiving the supportive well wishes and, when you feel a sense of that, blow out the first candle. Repeat the above steps for the present and the future, blowing out the second and then third candles.

This ritual is a reminder that the past, present and future are all happening *now* and that we have the power to influence each moment. A blessing to the past and the future is also an invitation to be here now.

WISH LISTS & LOVE LISTS RITUAL

Lists, lists, lists. Get into the habit of writing down all kinds of wish lists and love lists. Generally, I keep my lists anywhere from five to ten things, but do what feels good to you. When you feel you've finished, try to add a bonus one for good measure. I also feel it's important to start with love lists and then follow with wish lists. You can begin this in the wishing journal (page 136) and eventually keep your own separate wish journal. For your love lists, I suggest writing down things you love about your body, things you love about your past, things you love about your partner and things you love about the present moment. For wish lists, write wish lists for your home, your relationships, your work and your loved ones. These are just some suggestions. The main thing is to have fun with it, and to use writing these lists as a way to get your creative and motivational juices flowing. This infuses your wishes with the energy of permission and possibility.

WISH NOTES RITUAL

Write down wishes on notecards for people in your life that you are grateful for, and also for people who could use some extra support. If the wishes you choose align with any of the wishes in chapter four, you can use the wording given there. If not, you can come up with your own. When you're writing these wishes, begin by writing down what you can thank them for and then what you wish for them. As you write and wish, breathe in love and breathe out gratitude. Do this with the energy of abundance and generosity, without expecting anything in return.

Write down a wish note for someone that you don't know very well, and repeat the above.

Lastly write down a wish note for a stranger. If you like, you can hand it to them, or perhaps leave it on their seat as you leave the bus (it depends on how flirtatious you're feeling!).

This ritual is a reminder that, whatever you wish for another, you are wishing for yourself.

Write a letter to your 'shadow self' or your inner critic. Whatever needs to be said or communicated to your inner critic, write it down. Try to not censor it. However, do try to write the letter as if from the perspective of a loving parent, helper or healer.

Next, write a letter to someone you feel resentment or anger towards. Tell them how you feel; again, try not to censor yourself, but write from a place of advocacy and support rather than criticism.

After writing these letters, ceremoniously get rid of them. You can burn them or tear them up and throw them away. Take a few deep, cleansing breaths upon completion, breathing in freedom and breathing out love. (You may find you feel the need to hold on to the second letter and check in with yourself a month later to see if you actually need to send it to the person in question. That's entirely up to you. In some cases, that might bring great healing, but in others, not so much. This exercise is about letting go and strengthening the voice of your inner advocate. In some ways, it has nothing to do with the other person.)

THE WISHING HOUR

Once a week, set aside an hour and dedicate this time to your wishes and wish rituals. Take all your wish lists, wishing rituals, affirmations and inspirations and direct your own self-hypnosis mind movie. By that, I mean write down a master wish list and record yourself reciting it. State everything positively, in the present tense, and use a formula of praise and petition or command and appreciation. Spend time on your master wish list, rewriting it and keeping to simple, direct, affirmative statements and commands, for example, 'You are intelligent and you are receiving love and support for who you are and who you are becoming.' If the wishes you choose align with any of the wishes in chapter four, you can use the wording given there. If not, you can come up with your own. You will also find an example of a wishing hour script on pages 132–134.

Create your inspired space, call up your wishing mind and play your wishing music. Begin with one or two wishing rituals of your choice, then set a timer for about half an hour and lie back. Play the recording you have made of yourself reciting your master list. Allow the sound of your own voice and the words of your wishes to guide your wandering mind into a collaborative dreaming experience with your imagination, your subconscious mind and your best intentions.

Remember, there is no right or wrong way to do this. Your mind may wander and your thoughts may be busy or calm, relaxed or resistant. Just as in mediation, you can try to let your thoughts float by, but it's also OK to invite in an abundance of thoughts: just bring yourself back to the sound of your voice, or your breath or heartbeat, when you can.

If you don't want to record yourself, or you feel that listening
to your own voice is so strange that it distracts you, you
can write out your master list, read it through once silently,
then once aloud, and finally enter into your wishing mind.
Imagine that you are walking into a cinema. Look up at the
big screen and watch yourself on it, living as if your wishes
are coming true.

EVERYDAY WISHES

The practices shared here are small ways in which you can wish every day: simple practices that will help you create habits and enhance your wishing mind.

AFFIRMATIONS

When weaving your wishes into action, words are your friends. Write down your own affirmations and repeat them as often and as deeply as possible, every day. Take your list of things you love about yourself and your list of wishes for yourself and combine them to create your own affirmations. Combine one thing you appreciate about yourself and one thing you wish for yourself, and translate this into an affirmative statement. For example, 'I love that I'm generous' and 'I wish to fall in love' can be blended to create the affirmation: 'I love and appreciate my generosity and I am open and receptive to receiving the love of my life, trusting in myself and the process.'

The word 'affirmation' has its roots in the Latin '*ad firmare*', to strengthen or make firm. I've often heard affirmations getting a bad reputation for only working superficially. That's usually due to the absence of a true sense of the affirmation. When working with your affirmations, it's important to breathe them into your body and anchor them into an image or feeling using your senses. When we use affirmations in WishCraft, we go beyond words, figuratively and energetically 'casting' our intentions into action, like a spell. When we anchor the emotional association of the affirmation into our body with our imagination, it influences on a deeper level.

When starting out with affirmations, write at least ten and place them in a wishing bowl in your house. Choose one each day to work with. Repeat it to yourself when you are feeling joyful, and also when you are feeling down or neutral. Practise embodying it – this will give you a chance to monitor how it works and feels best for you, all the while reinforcing it.

GOOD NIGHT WISH

In the section on building appreciation (page 54), you began the practice of reviewing your day each night before you go to sleep, and thanking yourself for three things you did that day. Now we will expand on that. Once you have thanked yourself for those three things, repeat three words that describe how you want to feel or states of mind that you want to embody. Phrase it in a way that suggests you have already achieved these states of mind, for example: 'I feel confident, successful and attractive', or 'I am becoming more and more confident, successful and attractive every day'.

However you choose to say it, it's important that you *feel* it. Have fun with it and anchor it into a feeling state in your body. Say it three times before bed. When you wake up in the morning, look in the mirror and repeat it to yourself again, three times. As you stand in front of the mirror, you can look at yourself or look beyond yourself. Try imagining that you are looking at yourself through the eyes of someone who loves and appreciates you. If you don't want to say it in the mirror, you can say it (in your mind) while you brush your teeth or while you are having your morning coffee. The idea is to connect it to a habit, until the affirmation itself becomes a thought habit, and then a belief.

Looking back on your list of wishes, create a word or phrase of your year, for example: 'The year of surrender and abundance'. Write the phrase down somewhere where you can see it every day, perhaps the screensaver on your computer or the background on your phone, or somewhere where you spend a lot of time. Perhaps attach it to an inspiring photo that captures the vibe of how you want to feel. Whenever you need extra support, breathe into this phrase and really let yourself feel it.

PASSWORDS

Change your password to something that sums up one of your biggest wishes. Compose it affirmatively, imagining it coming true. Include the year in which you want it to come true or your lucky number, for example, '2020loveandmoney'. Every time you enter your password, you will be reinforcing your wish. Wishes become habits with repetition and reinforcement.

WISHING PLANT

Choose a plant to become your 'wishing plant' (see page 17 for the story of my own first wishing plant). Talk to it every day, and as you water it and nurture it, imagine that you are caring for it just as you are minding your wishes. If you happen to go on a long holiday and the plant starts to wilt, remember that your wishes are energy and have the ability to transcend and transform, so they can continue to work with you in another form. The wishing plant is a great way to focus on and care for our wishes and connect us to nature, patience and surrender.

WISHING WITH FRIENDS

Gather a group of well-wishing friends, admirers and inspiring people who you feel excited to conspire with and who you feel will help to hold your wishes accountable to the world. This will work like a sacred well-wishing manifestation circle. Ideally, you will meet once a week or twice a month for three to six months and work your wishes together. You can perform wishing rituals and exercises together and end each circle with a wishing ceremony. I suggest you open the circle by checking in with each other and sharing how you feel, then working through a few rituals, exercises and wishes, before closing the circle by declaring your wishes and sharing appreciation. If the wishes you choose align with any of the wishes in chapter four, you can use the wording given there. If not, you can come up with your own.

Here are some group wishing exercises you can try together.

OPENING THE CIRCLE

Choose a positive invocation to recite together to open your wishing circle, for example the one on page 107.

MOOD BOARD

Write out your wishes, then take some old magazines and books and cut out pictures, words, phrases and colours that seem to connect to your wishes. Create a collage using your cuttings and images with the intention of capturing or creating the mood of your future vision (which is why it is sometimes called a vision board).

This is an intuitive and fun process, meant to bypass the conscious, critical mind and tap into the genius of the free-wheeling subconscious mind. Just as the affirmations go deeper when truly felt, the vision goes deeper when it's a mood or state of mind you are embodying and moving into, as opposed to a material concept you are getting attached to – so you will find that images that summon up a certain feeling will be more impactful than an image of a particular car or house that you want. You can place your mood board somewhere prominent where you see it often and feel inspired by it, or, if that's not your style, place it somewhere private, where you can check in with it every now and then, connecting with your mood board as an intuitive GPS to help you drive in the direction of your dreams.

This activity also works well as a solo activity, but doing it in a group creates a sense of collaboration and sharing.

'EXQUISITE CORPSE' COLLECTIVE MANIFESTATION

Once used as parlour game of the Dadaist and Surrealist artists, the 'exquisite corpse' exercise is another great trick to bypass the conscious mind and expand into free association collective consciousness.

On a sheet of paper, write down two wishes: a wish for yourself and a wish for the world. Fold the paper to cover the first sentence and pass the paper on to the next person. They will only see the wish for the world. They must write two wishes inspired by that sequence (again, one wish for themselves and one for the world), then fold over the paper once again so that only the last wish is visible. Continue passing the paper around and adding wishes in this manner until you have at least eight wishes. When you're finished, one person reads the list aloud. It's an experimental way to glimpse the collective consciousness, to connect our wishes for ourselves to one another, and to develop a collective vision for the future.

Use the circle to hold yourself accountable: commit to starting (or even finishing) a project before the next time the circle meets. Sign yourself up for that class you've been wanting to try, plan your art exhibit, go on that date. Whatever it is, make sure you commit to it and follow through with the circle as your witness.

CLOSING THE CIRCLE

Always remember that, whatever you wish for another, you are wishing for yourself. The circle reminds us that creativity thrives in collaboration and the Universe rewards commitment.

At the closing of each circle, don't forget to recite together, three times: 'Just as I wish well for myself, may your wishes come true.'

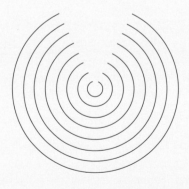

*Just as I wish well
for myself, may your
wishes come true.*

*Just as I wish well
for myself, may your
wishes come true.*

*Just as I wish well
for myself, may your
wishes come true.*

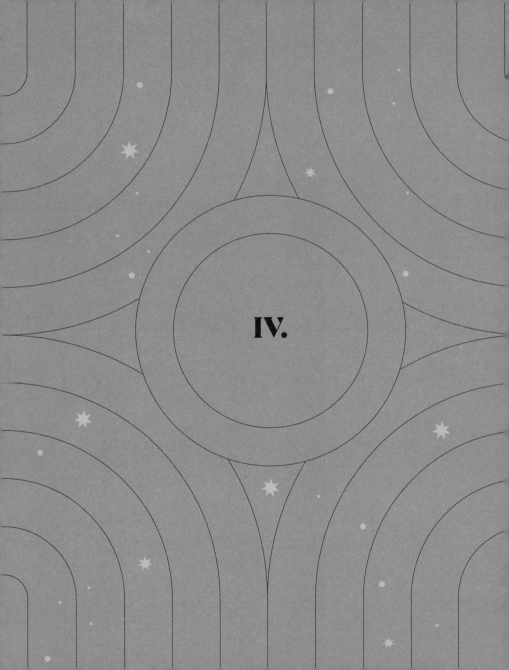

IV.

THE
WISHES

THE WISHES

In this chapter, I am sharing a variety of long wishes, blessings and affirmations for you to work with in your WishCraft. My hope is that you work with these wishes as blessings to comfort and guide you through changes and challenges that you may experience during the different phases of your life. May these wishes awaken an intimacy between yourself and your dreams, strengthening your relationship with the wishing well of possibility within you.

While there is no right or wrong way to work with wishes, and you will, ultimately, find a way that works for you, my suggestion is that you work with these wishes in the rhythm of relaxing, releasing and receiving. I suggest keeping this sequence in mind as it facilitates the energy of perceiving, believing and receiving, which I will explain below.

After following the instructions and exercises at the start of the book in order to cultivate your wishing state of mind, you can begin by choosing to work with the one or two wishes at a time, beginning with the exercises in 'Cultivating your practice' (pages 67–81) and the wishing rituals (pages 83–88) and working up to the wishing hour (pages 132–134). Monitor your own progress and journal about what's coming up for you as you go. As with any transformation, there are bound to be uncomfortable moments. I encourage you to take it slowly and look at what you're feeling through a lens of curiosity.

The wishes should be said like prayers, affirmations, and blessings, and experienced like meditations and hypnotic reprogrammings all in one. I have divided the wishes into three sections: wishes to heal (prayers); wishes to give (blessings); and finally, wishes to receive (affirmations).

As you move through your WishCraft journey, remember the mantra I shared with you earlier: 'Perceive, believe, receive'. Take a few moments to let the deeper meaning behind this mantra really sink into your whole body and mind. Soon, 'Perceive, believe, receive' will be running through you, effortlessly.

PERCEIVE

When we are in a state of trance or relaxation, we can begin to perceive things more clearly.

BELIEVE

When we bring our attention to our resources and begin to collaborate with the parts of us that need support, we can begin to shift our beliefs and holistically influence ourselves on a deeper level, helping us to believe that our wishes will come true.

RECEIVE

When we increase our self-worth with compassion and appreciation for ourselves and begin to imagine and believe in what's possible, we can bring our imagination to life. In the spirit of fun, curiosity and collaboration, we begin to take inspired action, surrendering to the process of receiving what we perceive and believe.

As I mentioned earlier, I use what I call 'hypno-poetic licence' in the language I choose for my wishes, which I assume you have already taken a note of. This is a very intentional choice when it comes to wishes, self-hypnosis and especially WishCraft. The best hypnotic language is 'artfully vague', in the style of the great North American hypnotist Milton Erickson. There is a saying in hypnosis: 'Don't step on my trance, man'. Using artfully vague language allows space to fill in its true desires with the artistry of its own unique genius. One such statement that I repeat often in my wishes is 'Positive present future now'. This is hypno-poetic language for saying that it's all happening now. Imagining a positive future allows you to experience it now in your mind.

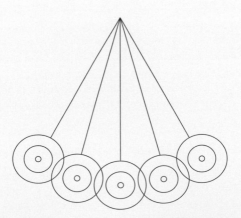

INVOCATION: RELAXING, RELEASING & RECEIVING

This invocation should be repeated throughout the wishing process. I encourage you to say it often at the beginning of your wishing practice and whenever you need support: it will lay the foundations for a comfortable, supportive environment, and can be remembered and repeated if any difficult feelings arise. It also works well as a ritual incantation for invoking your wishing circles.

I am relaxing, releasing and receiving, just breathing. Trusting in myself and enjoying the process of expanding into my positive present future now. In the direction of my highest good, I surrender to the supportive forces within me and around me. I am moving forwards positively, just being me.

WISHES FOR HEALING

To be said like prayers, petitioning for divine guidance or help from your higher self. Alternatively, you could read aloud, record and play back to yourself, for ease. I have also recorded these wishes, which you can find on my website, shaunacummins.com.

INNER CHILD

I wish for healing and release for my inner child. I wish to send healing for and release from any suffering my inner child has experienced. May my inner child receive the healing and support that they needed, even if just in the 'medicine of my imagination' now. May they find healing for the things that no one apologised for. May they feel loved and supported in whatever way makes sense for them now. May this healing and release flow freely through me now and into my inner child. May my future, present and past selves collaborate in my healing process now. Learning and growing and becoming stronger. In my own way and in my own time. Thank you for my positive present future now.

NOTE   You have many inner children, toddlers, teenagers, young adults, etc. You can use this prayer for each one of them when you need them most. Remember to be tender and gentle with your inner child. Ask for their permission to be with them and help them to heal, establishing a safe, secure and protected relationship with them that will continue to grow.

I wish for healing for my inner critic. I wish for them to feel safe enough to surrender judgement and expectation in the interests of learning and growing stronger. I wish for my inner critic to have the courage to be vulnerable enough to let go and to give way to the healing and transformation that is available to them now. I thank my inner critic for giving in to the humility of healing and release that allow me to become who I really am now.

Trusting in myself and enjoying the process of learning and growing and becoming stronger. Thank you for my positive present future now.

FORGIVENESS

I wish for healing and forgiveness for myself. I wish to send healing and forgiveness to the parts of me stuck in past resentments, regrets and heartbreaks. May I feel free to move forwards with courage and curiosity, trusting in myself and the process of healing and releasing. May I find an intuitive balance in the practice of advocating for myself and letting go of what no longer serves me.

May I get better and better at seeing and believing that I am not what happened to me; I am what I choose to become. May I forgive myself for the times I froze in fear, for the times I forgot my power and my worth.

I trust each step forwards is working with me, in my own way and my own time. Growing stronger, becoming more open and receptive to the supportive forces within me and around me. Thank you for my positive present future now.

I wish for healing for myself and release from regret. I wish to learn from and let go of past mistakes, transforming the regret into acceptance, the acceptance into knowledge and the knowledge into freedom: freedom to express greater love towards myself and my life, freedom to just be me. May I find the humbleness to admit regret, knowing that I am learning and growing and becoming stronger, more open and receptive to the infinite field of possibilities. I take responsibility for my past mistakes, learning and growing, as I move forwards wiser and stronger. Thank you for my positive present future now.

MONEY

I wish for healing for myself around scarcity or lack. I wish for an allowing and deserving mindset of abundance, to become more open and receptive to money flowing easily to me. May I clear out and release any old blocks or tensions around money that no longer serve me. May I return those limiting beliefs or thoughts around money to wherever they came from, with forgiveness and release. May I realise freedom now, becoming free to express greater love and support towards who I am and who I am becoming, just breathing. Giving and receiving, easily and abundantly. May I feel my future self here with me, enjoying financial freedom and success.

Surrendering to the supportive forces within me and around me. Thank you for my positive present future now.

I wish for the healing of my body and the release of any past traumas it may be holding on to, whether from myself, other people or society. I wish for a healthy body and wellbeing. May I send healing and relief to any past parts struggling with health or love for my body. May I send thanks to my body for always being there for me: my breath, my blood, my heartbeat – each and every part of me that supports me, every minute of every day. I send love and appreciation and I feel the harmony flowing through my awareness, bringing my body into alignment. I experience my future self, healthy and here with me now. Thank you for what my body is now and what it can be, learning and growing and becoming stronger. Surrendering to the supportive forces within me and around me. Trusting in myself and enjoying the process, in my own way and in my own time. Thank you for my positive present future now.

ANCESTORS

I wish for the healing and release of my ancestors. I thank them and I sense their ability to overcome and survive. I imagine what they appreciate about my life now. Receiving that appreciation, I send gratitude to them. Sensing my freedom now, I honour their hardships and struggles, their skills and abilities, by wishing well for myself now. Surrendering to the supportive forces within me and around me. When I think of myself, I think of someone who is learning and growing and becoming stronger. Trusting in myself and enjoying the process. Thank you for my positive present future now.

WISHES FOR GIVING

The following wishes are to be read silently, or spoken out loud as blessings.

SELF-CONFIDENCE TO CHANGE

May I give myself the power to rewrite my own story. May I choose to step into something new and more aligned with my authentic truth. May I navigate transformation with grace and expand into my true potential. May I give myself permission and encouragement to be confident just being me.

LOVE

May I give love and acceptance to myself, deeply and completely. May I live receiving unconditional love for who I was, who I am and who I am becoming. May I give love to myself in sickness and in health, for worse and for better. May I give to myself the effort and actions of love that I give to other people, experiencing myself as my own loved one now. May I give and receive love easily and abundantly. May I love and accept myself completely, just the way I am.

SUCCESS

May I give to myself the chance to focus clearly, so that I may move forwards into my power. May I give myself the support and encouragement that I didn't have when I needed it, knowing that the possibility for a new future and a new perspective on the past are always available to me. May I give myself the patience and discipline to learn new skills and abilities. May I succeed just being me.

May I give myself space and support to allow my creative life-force energy to flow positively within me and around me, allowing that energy to find form in my talents, passions and abilities. May I fulfil my purpose. May my soul be inspired to act in a way that will channel my creativity and serve with purpose and passion.

BODY

May I give love and appreciation to my body and feel harmony flowing through my awareness, bringing my body into alignment with my best intentions. May I experience my future self as a healthy body, nourished with love and support in habit and mind, finding a balance of focus and forgiveness, moving forwards positively. May I cultivate habits that support life-giving energies to circulate within me and around me. May I tend to my body with even half as much appreciation and love as she gives me in every cell, every second of every day. May I be present here with my body now, like a loved one, in gratitude and appreciation, thanking my body for what it is now and what it is becoming.

COMMUNITY

May I give to my community positive actions in an effort to contribute towards our greater good and collective future. May I experience the Universe giving me many opportunities to serve a greater purpose. I am grateful to have a part in the healing of our group consciousness. I look forward to the everyday ways in which I can be of service to myself and others.

May I give of myself in order to help the world (the people, animals and plants that inhabit it), and to sense its natural intelligence to survive and grow stronger. I wish for the world (the people, animals and plants that inhabit it) to come together, remembering and awakening the constellation of cosmic energy that connects us all. Surrendering to the innate healing powers of nature, may the world and its inhabitants begin to harmonise in the way of healing, learning and growing stronger now. Thank you for what it is and what it can be.

EARTH

May I give gratitude and appreciation to the Earth for her bounty, wisdom and dynamic force. May I bow in humility and surrender to her generative strength and life-giving resources. May I honour the Earth as a living, breathing thing, just as myself, with care and compassion. May I honour and respect the rhythms of nature and fragility of life. May I exercise awareness and flexibility so that my habits and actions are in alignment with preserving her resources with reverence and regard for her future.

May I give space and time to listen closely to the whispers of my spirit and the spirits around me, paying close attention to the unique language of my senses giving voice to my spirit. Listening to my breath, may I hear the fullness of the spirit within me. Trusting in myself and the process. Thank you for the wisdom and guidance that have been with me throughout my whole life and that will continue to guide me.

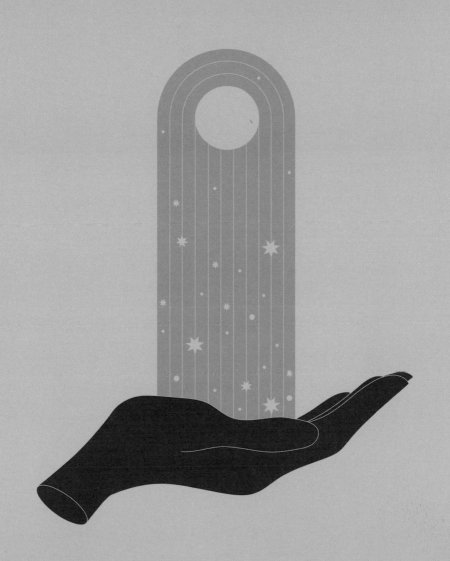

WISHES TO RECEIVE

To be said and read as affirmations.

LOVE & BELONGING

I now claim my wish for love and belonging and bring it into action. I am thankful and enjoying an intimate sense of feeling at home in my body, in my relationships and in the world. I now feel safe, secure and protected, no matter what has happened in the past, remembering what I know now: that this love and belonging have been with me throughout my whole life and they are awakened now; that I can share this belonging in a loving, romantic partnership, remembering how strong, resourceful and supported I really am, just being me. This love now flows easily into all the places within me that need comfort from loneliness and wounding. Feeling my breath as my medicine and my natural ability to ground myself in my body, just breathing. Trusting in this sense of belonging to unfold even deeper within me and around me as I feel my future supporting me now. Belonging here now, in loving, supportive relationships with myself and my loved ones. I thank you for my positive present future now.

I now claim my wish for receiving an abundance mindset, believing I can have what I truly desire now. I bring this wish into action, allowing myself to receive my desire. I now release and dissolve all the webs of resistances within me, receiving even more of what I wish for now. Trusting in myself and the process, I feel love and support flowing easily to and from me. I thank the parts of me that have already received what I desire.

Trusting in myself and my natural ability to shift, to let go and to receive even more of what I desire now. I give myself even more of what I need now, just being me. Thank you for my positive present future now.

INNER PEACE & FULFILMENT

I now claim my wish for finding a sense of peace within me and bring it into action. I now enjoy a peacefulness within myself, despite whatever is going on around me, so that I may expand into the inner reservoir of resources inside me: the infinite ability to heal, to let go and to receive even more of what I need now. May I open myself even more deeply now to my senses and my natural ability to slow down, to listen and to receive what I need to feel peace now. I thank myself for acknowledging, honouring and integrating myself into peacefulness, just being me. Thank you for my positive present future now.

I now claim my wish for expanding my generosity of spirit,
opening myself to the freedom of giving freely what I wish
and what I wish for others. May I trust in myself and my
ability to expand into giving, transcending the mind traps
of comparison and envy.

Trusting in the abundance of the Universe, and the
divine guidance of my own path. Giving way to the natural
ability of the mind, body and spirit to live fully and abundantly
here, now. Giving in to the energy within us and around
us. Thank you for the positive present future now.

COURAGE & STRENGTH

I now claim my wish for courage and bring it into action.
I now have the courage to grow stronger as I move through
my life, surrendering my wishes into action. I breathe
into my heart and expand into my courage, just being me,
allowing myself to expand into my potential. I thank my
future self for supporting me in remembering how strong,
resourceful and in control I really am, trusting in myself and
the inner intelligence of my mind and body, to know exactly
how to grow, how to let go and how to move into action. May
I find possibility and support in my imagination by letting
go of the outcome and enjoying the process of learning and
growing stronger, taking risks with confidence and adjusting
easily. Thank you for my positive present future now.

I now claim my wish for the creative life-force energy within me and around me to begin to harmonise my desires into action. I send support to all past parts of me that needed nourishment and I give myself permission and encouragement to take action now, with an intuitive balance of focus and support. I allow my creative life-force energy to express itself fully in me now, in my work, awakening my talents as offerings into the world. Tuning into the creativity in nature, in my body, in my mind and spirit, trusting in myself and the process of creating. I thank my creativity for flowing through me now like a channel of light and energy. Trusting in myself and enjoying the process of learning and growing and becoming stronger. Thank you for my positive present future now.

WISHES FOR DIFFERENT STAGES & PHASES

THE DAY

I wish for my day to begin at ease and finish at peace, trusting in myself and the magic of new beginnings, no matter what's going on within me and around me. Allowing good things to come to me and to let go of all that is not meant for me, believing in myself and the process of learning and growing and becoming stronger. I imagine my wish for the day coming true for me and can feel it now as if it's already happened. Trusting in myself and enjoying the process. Thank you for what it is and what it can be.

THE YEAR

I wish for my year to begin with light and energy, just as the sun rises at dawn, full of potential and fire to bring my dreams into action. Just as seeds grow into flowers, I believe in my wishes coming to fruition for the greater good of myself and the world. May my wishes for this year come true in light of the highest good for me, others and the world. I am trusting in myself and enjoying the process. Learning and growing and becoming stronger in my own way and in my own time. Thank you for what it is and what it can be.

I wish for my home to be a place of warmth, a place where
I may feel safe and nourished, a place to sleep, eat and
tend to the intimate matters of my life. May it be protected
and blessed with the energy that I wish for it. May I invite
whoever I wish to share this warmth, wonder and joy. May
it be a place to nourish, ground and support me. Thank you
for what it is and what it can be.

NEW RELATIONSHIP

I wish for my relationship to move in the direction of my
highest good, for my learning and growing, giving and
receiving. May I have the courage to move through any
fear or resistance with compassion and patience, allowing
a healthy, supportive relationship now. Trusting in myself
and the process. Surrendering to the supportive forces within
me and around me. Learning and growing and becoming
stronger. Thank you for what it is and what it can be.

I wish for confidence and prosperity as I expand into my potential. May my unique gifts and talents find a way to express their purpose in fulfilment of the greatest good for myself, others and the world. Trusting in myself and the process. I know that things take time and effort to achieve, but I feel positive and supported, knowing each step forwards is working with me, in my own way and in my own time. Surrendering to the supportive forces within me and around me. Thank you for what it is and what it can be.

NEW MOON

I wish to surrender my true desires to the rhythms of the cosmic will and the power of the Universe in order to manifest my highest potential. Trusting in myself and the process, just as the waves trust the push and pull of the Moon. I return to my breath, breathing in and out, feeling my breath and desires in rhythm with the waves, gliding in and out. I trust in myself and the cosmic will and power of the Universe to manifest my desires and make my future dreams reality now. Trusting in myself and the process of manifesting my wishes in accordance with my highest good, and moving forwards positively. Thank you for what it is and what it can be.

WISHES
FOR REVOLUTION

To be said like confessions, admitting to the wrongdoings
of ourselves and others, in atonement or with the intention
of coming into alignment with right action.

FOR THE EARTH

May I awaken to recognise the Earth as a living organism,
May I treat her like a divine mother and giver of life: the
ocean's water, the trees' air, the soil's growth. May I begin
to live my life by right actions to sustain a living future.

FOR NEIGHBOURS

May I stand together with my neighbours to create positive
collective change for all. I believe in the goodness of the
world and its people. Together we can move forward
positively. I believe in the power of our voices, actions,
and love to create positives together.

May I stand with love and respect for all life. May I listen, learn and act with compassion. May I embody the humility to admit when I am wrong and make reparations for deep, lasting, systemic change towards equality on all levels. May I learn to see others and myself as one, with generosity and grace.

CLOSING WISH

To be used at the end of a wish to close it out energetically – sort of like 'sealing your wish with a kiss'. In all my wishing, may I have the patience to let go of what no longer serves my highest good, moving like a river flows, surrendering to the supportive slipstreams, moving forwards positively, just being me. Trusting in myself and the process of learning and growing and becoming stronger, and more open and receptive to making my future dreams a reality now.

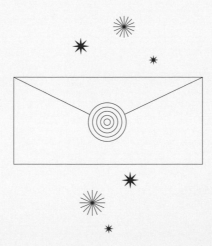

WISHING HOUR: DEEP MIND WISHING

A script to be read aloud in a group (such as the wishing circle) or to be read aloud to yourself before entering into a wishing trance. Alternatively, you can record it and listen to it before you go to sleep or before you enter into the wishing trance or journey.

PAST PRESENT FUTURE NOW: UPDATING THE OPERATING SYSTEM TO THE QUANTUM FIELD

Imagining myself in a peaceful place, I breathe in deep relaxation into my mind and into my body. Counting down from ten to one, breathing slowly and deeply. Ten, nine, eight, breathing, seven, six, five, deeper and deeper, four, three, two, one; allowing each and every breath to take me deeper into this intuitive inner space for relaxation and release, receiving even more of what I desire now. Breathing in relaxation and breathing out release. Breathing in, deeper and deeper, into the intuitive inner space of the mind and body. Safe, secure and protected, just breathing. Remembering that, in my mind, I can give myself whatever resources I need: the ability to go deeper, to rise above and to give myself what I need, is my natural ability.

Now, in my mind, I find myself somewhere that brings me peace, a place in nature. I am experiencing this place with all of my senses. The colour of the sky, the sounds around me, the temperature of the air on my skin. Breathing in peacefulness and support. Drawing up courage and strength from the earth and into my body, into my mind, light and clarity from the sun and the sky moving into my mind, into my body. I experience those energies circulating throughout my body, empowering me to move forwards positively.

I now imagine myself from the perspective of my future self. I can feel or see my future self doing well, living, their wishes coming true. I step into my future self, moving around in their energy, feeling it now. I believe in myself; I trust in myself; I feel my whole mind and my whole body working with me now.

Through the eyes of my future self, I can see my present self and I notice what I admire about my present self now. I feel my present self receiving that appreciation. I can feel those energies, from the future and the present, collaborating, working together and rising up and intuitively travelling over my life. I can look down as if I'm looking down from above, and I call out a few things I feel very proud of, things I accomplished or overcame throughout my life.

When I have those in mind, I drop down and travel to the past, to a time when I could have used more support. And I feel my future and present selves there with my past self as if I'm my own loved one or my own best friend. I give my past self whatever resources I needed, and I imagine my past self receiving those resources: protection, healing, safety. I look into the eyes of my past self and I remind them of or share with them what I admire about them. I share with them what they will go on to accomplish or overcome. I feel pathways of healing, releasing and receiving, flowing from the future into the present, into the past, and I can feel my past self now rising up out of that past, feeling an updated sense of love and support for who they are and who they are becoming; travelling through time and space with an updated sense of love and support for who they are and who they are becoming.

I can feel myself in the present moment, moving forwards positively, and I can feel my future self here with me now, supporting me. Moving forwards, in my own way and in my own time, remembering how strong, resourceful and supported I really am, just being me. Enjoying myself and the process, in my own way and in my time. I know that things take time and energy to accomplish, but I now feel an intuitive balance of focus and forgiveness, trusting in myself and the process. Each step forwards works with me, surrendering to the supportive forces within me and around me. Thank you for my positive present future now. My future dreams are a reality now.

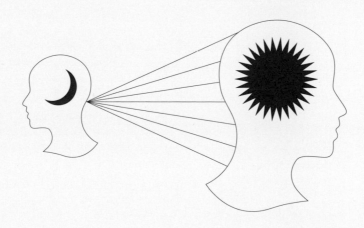

V.

WISHING
JOURNAL

The following pages have been
left blank for you to begin writing
your own wishes. Just as with the
wishes on the preceding pages, you
can dip in and out of your personal
wishes, calling upon them as and
when you need them, and eventually
progressing to an entirely separate
wishing journal. Half of the pages are
for wishes for yourself, and the other
half are wishes for someone else.

MY WISH

MY WISH

MY WISH

MY WISH

MY WISH

MY WISH

MY WISH FOR YOU

MY WISH FOR YOU

MY WISH FOR YOU

MY WISH FOR YOU

MY WISH FOR YOU

MY WISH FOR YOU

AFTERWORD

I remember many moons ago, when I was travelling the desert in India with an ex-boyfriend. I was uncomfortable and tired, feeling like a piece of tattered sandpaper flopping in the wind. (The way one does after sleeping out in the desert for days without a tent.) Looking out of the train window at the wild colours of the land sweeping by in blurry lines, and in that liminal space of discomfort and fear, suddenly, like a pin hole to the ocean, a door of energy burst open up within me. Waves of immense gratitude came flooding through my senses; waves of remembering all of the kind people who had helped me along my way; waves of images of loved ones; flashbacks of strangers' eyes offering support; my father's unconditional patience with me; the ones who forgave me, and who believed in me even when I didn't; the ones who were genuinely happy for me when good things happened regardless of what was in it for them.

Of course I knew that it was always there, but for that moment all the fear flooded out; all the pain and the unworthiness disappeared and I was filled up with a Love Supreme. This amazing energy reconnected me to a devotional vow that I have been in service to ever since: to honour and to love too much and to do it anyway, not for me or you, but for us.

As our time together comes to an end, in recognition of privilege, and in acknowledgment of trauma, I invite you to rise up in your wishing practice and to actively choose love.We are all in this together, with the birds and the bees and the trees. It may not always be wishes and kisses, but when we can wish, and when we can kiss, let's make it good and deep and strong.

Like my train ride, this book has been an invitation to move between different levels of consciousness, and I hope that you are in a different place now, than when we began.

In hypnosis, and in most spiritual traditions, it is understood that we exist at many different levels of consciousness, and that we move between these levels of awareness many times throughout the day. With WishCraft, this simply becomes a conscious act.

We often take for granted the idea of a mood or a feeling. But imagine walking down the street on a gloomy day, and suddenly you run into someone you LOVE who you haven't seen in forever ... and suddenly your whole being shifts and you are happy, and feeling good.

This is how simple it can be to manifest a positive future NOW. As we part ways, the main thing to remember is that wishing and crafting and making your dreams come true is a CREATIVE ACT. You are in collaboration with different parts of you to make your dreams come true. You are the one who creates the life you want to live and who has agency over your reality. So please use your feelings, thoughts and actions like a painter would use paint and a paintbrush. These are your tools. This is your W.I.S.H. This is your C.R.A.F.T. Use it to make lots of wishes!

Just as I wish well for myself,
may your wishes come true.

Love, Shauna

ACKNOWLEDGEMENTS

This wish of a book, would not have come to be, without the love and support of many a wishing mind. Thank you first to my family. To my mother, the late Hannah Brosnan Cummins and to my father Larry Cummins, for their legendary generosity and unconditional love, for always wanting the best for me and doing everything they could to give me the opportunities they never had. Thank you to my sister Kelly for her unwavering enthusiasm, fierce protection and all the laughs. Thank you to my brother Eamonn for introducing me to a larger world of possibility through story and art and for the shared love of our Irish heritage. Thank you to my nieces and nephew for the honour of watching them grow into their unique talents and virtues. To Hannah for her fortitude, to Grace for her sincerity, to Jaqueline for her style, to Brendan for his keen perception and Devyn for her tenacity. For my godmother, Tracie and my sister-in-law Kim for supporting and encouraging me in my spiritual sensibilities.

Thank you to all my soul friends around the world. To Kelly Mckay, for her true presence and remarkable compassion. To Lily Benson, for her bright magic and generous mind. To Yvonne Cullen, for her timeless sensitivity and poetic reverence for the unseen world. To Morgan Yakus for her sharp intuition, deep empathy and hypnotic sisterhood. To Sebastian Sadowski, for seeing me through thick and thin and always wishing me well, and for proving that you don't have to be organised to be successful. To Michelle Cade for her kindness and collaborations. To Sushma Sagar for her elegance and adventurous spirit. For Mammamoon a.k.a. Semra Haksever, for making this WishCraft book a dream come true!

To my NY girl gang of mamas, mystics, activists and artists, thank you for your friendship and support through all the ups and downs to Anya Ferring, Amber Milanovich, Samantha Yurkosky, Danniele Swatosh, Maria Margolies, Dorothee Senechal, Debbie Attias, Erika Spring, Ewa Joseffsson, Emma Andrea, AniBerberian, Christina Clare, Dalila Pasotti, Eliza Traina, Hillary Keel, Catie Casano, Laura Craft, Lovisa Ringborg and Kira Byelina.

To my hypnosis mentor and teacher Melissa Tiers for her fierce integrity and unconditional support and for paving the brave way for women like me on the hypnosis path. To the late Gary Brown, Jungian therapist and lay buddhist priest, for creating a safe enough space to feel my anger with courage and compassion. To Lisa Levine and the Maha Rose family for being the original spirit doula for the WishCraft. To Jill Urwin and Cheryl Isabel and the entire SLC crew for making WishCraft international! And Laurie Henzel and BUST Magazine for being so righteous.

And to the most understanding and encouraging team at Hardie Grant, to my editor Eve Marleau for being endlessly easy and inspiring to work with. To Kate Pollard for commissioning this book and believing in the vision of WishCraft.

And last, but definitely not least, to my two wordsmith fairy godmothers, who both swooped in to save the day in their own way. To Kristin Prevallet for her editor's eye and hypno-poetic expertise. Ruby Warrington for her incisive and surgical edits, tempered with encouragement and patience.

And, of course, one more encore thank you, to all The Divine Feminine Hypnotists who have trusted me to guide them into this mind field, it's an honor and an inspiration.

ABOUT THE AUTHOR

Shauna Cummins is a professional hypnotist and multidisciplinary artist. She is the founder of the Divine Feminine School of Hypnosis and The WishCraft. The WishCraft is a method of self-hypnosis that teaches the art of well-wishing as a practice for changing thought patterns and beliefs, turning wishes into action. She teaches workshops, holds ceremonies, creates hypnotic sound art and installations. She holds a private hypnosis practice in New York City at the Center for Integrative Hypnosis. Her work has been featured internationally at The National Gallery of Denmark, The Queens Museum of New York, The Center for Contemporary Art Glasgow and in publications such as the Independent, YAHOO news and The Numinous among others. She lives in the woods in upstate New York in a magical healing house that has three wishing wells with her cat Suki, a.k.a. The WishCat.

156

A

abundance mindset 71
    abundance mindset wish 121
action, creativity & action wish 123
affirmations 93–4, 97, 103
ancestors, wishes for 112
animal magnetism 44
appreciation 54, 65, 67, 70, 71, 77, 94
Artemis 49

B

birthdays, candles and 49
the body
    wish of appreciation towards 116
    wish for healing of 112
Brahman 68
Brigid, St 46
Buddhism, loving-kindness meditation 77–8

C

Cameron, Julia 77–8
candles
    birthday cakes and 49
    candle ritual 86
career, wish for a new job or 127
Celtic traditions 22, 44
    wishing wells 45
changework 31–8, 43
    self-confidence to change wish 115
Chinese philosophy 45
circles, wishing 96–8
closing wish 130
community 53, 58, 67
    community manifestation 98
    wish for community 116
compassion 29, 53, 55, 67, 77, 78
Cornish traditions 49
courage & strength wish 122

creativity 53, 56, 67
    creativity & action wish 123
    wishes for 116, 123
curiosity 53, 57

D

Dada 97
dandelions 51
the day, wish for 125
daydreams 22
deep mind wishing 132–4
dopamine 38, 71

E

Earth, wishes for the 117, 129
Egyptians
    Egyptian sleeping temples 22
    hypnosis 43–4
11:11 51
envy, generosity & overcoming
  envy wish 122
equality, wish for 129
Erikson, Milton 105
everyday wishes 93–5
    affirmations 93–4
    good night wish 94
    passwords 95
    phrase of the year 95
    wishing plants 95
'exquisite corpse' collective
  manifestation 97
eyelashes 49

F

farmers, ladybirds and 50
forgiveness, wish for 110
friends, wishing with 96–9
fulfilment, inner peace & fulfilment wish 121

G

Ganges, India 45
generosity & overcoming
  envy wish 122
Germanic traditions 22
giving, wishes for 115–18
good night wish 94
gratitude 60, 71
Greeks, candles
  and birthday cakes 49

H

healing, wishes for 109–12
Hindu mythology 68
home, wish for a new 126
hypnagogic state 22
hypnosis 22
  history of 43–6

I

imagination 24, 25–9, 56, 65, 68
  time-travelling in your 72
Imbolc 46
inner child 20, 76
  healing wish for 109
inner critic 76, 88
  healing wish for 110
inner peace
  & fulfilment wish 121
invocation, relaxing, releasing
  & receiving 106–7
Ireland, wishing trees 83

J

jealousy 77–8
job, wish for a new 127
journals, wishing 136–51

L

ladybirds 50
language, hypnotic 105
The Law of Attraction 26, 29, 71
Lee, Bruce 45
letting go 88
lists, wish lists & love lists ritual 86–7
Lourdes, France 45
love
  love & belonging wish 120
  love lists & wish lists ritual 86–7
  loving-kindness meditation 77–8
  wish for 115
  wish for a new relationship 126

M

mantra, 'perceive, believe, receive' 20,
  104
meditation 22, 43
  loving-kindness meditation 77–8
Mesmer, Franz Anton 44
mind, the wishing 24
money, wish for 111
mood boards 96–7
moon, wish for a new 127

N

neural pathways, creating new 31
neuroplasticity 31, 68
new moon, wish for a 127
numbers, repeating 51

O

oneness 80
Ono, Yoko, *Wishing Tree* 83
Overdurf, John 75
overview effect 65

158

P

parts therapy 75
passwords 95
past present future now wish 132–4
patience 67
peace, inner peace
  & fulfilment wish 121
'perceive, believe, receive' mantra 20, 104
phrase of the year 95
Placebo effect 44
plants, wishing 95
play and playfulness 68
prayer 22
Ptolemy 50

R

receiving, wishes
  to receive 120–3
regret, wish for 111
relationships, wish for new 126
relaxation
  deep relaxation 22
  releasing & receiving
    invocation 106–7
reparations, wish for 130
repetition
  and receptiveness
    to suggestion 54
  repeating numbers 51
resentment 77, 78, 88
revolution, wishes for 129–30
rituals, wishing 83–8, 96
  candle ritual 86
  ritual washing 84
  shadow healing ritual 88
  wish lists & love lists ritual 86–7
  wish notes ritual 87
  wishing bowl ritual 85

S

savasana 22
the self 75
self-appreciation 70
self-collaboration 53, 54, 67
self-confidence to change wish 115
self-hypnosis, understanding 11–12
serotonin 38, 71
shadow healing ritual 88
Shamanic ceremonies 22
shooting stars 50
spirits, wishes for 118
stars 50
strength, courage
  & strength wish 122
success, wish for 115
suggestibility 22–4
surprise 57
Surrealists 97

T

thanking yourself 54
thoughts 65
  and art of manifesting 29–30
  changing thought patterns 31
  number of a day 26
transformation 43
Trevi Fountain, Rome 45

V

Virgin Mary 50
vision boards 96–7

W

washing, ingredients for ritual 84
water 45–6, 47

wells, wishing 22, 44, 83–4
  origins of 45
Wilde, Oscar 68
wish lists & love lists ritual 86–7
wish notes ritual 87
wishcraft 36–7
  cultivating your practice 67–81
  cultural traditions 48–51
  definition of 11–12
  everyday wishes 93–5
  finding your wishing mind 60
  foundations of 41–61
  pillars of 53–9
  ways to wish 62–99
  wishing mind 24, 29–30
  wishing for others 75–80
  wishing others well with loving-
    kindness 77
  wishing rituals 83–8, 96
  wishing well for other parts
    of yourself 75–6
  wishing well for someone you'll
    never meet 80–1
  wishing with friends 96–9
  wishing for the world
    or community 80–1
  wishing for yourself 70–3
wishes 100–34
  abundance mindset wish 121
  for the body 112, 116
  closing wish 130
  for community 116
  courage & strength wish 122
  for creativity 116
  creativity & action wish 123
  for the day 125
  deep mind wishing 132–4
  for different stages & phases 125–7
  for the Earth 117, 129
  for equality 129
  for forgiveness 110
  generosity & overcoming
    envy wish 122
  giving wishes 115–18
  healing wishes 109–12
  for inner child 109
  for inner critic 110
  inner peace & fulfilment wish 121
  for love 115
  love & belonging wish 120
  for money 111
  for my ancestors 112
  for a new home 126
  for a new job or career 127
  for a new moon 127
  for new relationships 126
  for regret 111
  for reparations 130
  for revolution 129–30
  self-confidence to change wish 115
  for spirits 118
  for success 115
  wishes to receive 120–3
  for the world 117
  for the year 125
wishing bowls 83–4
  wishing bowl ritual 85
wishing circles
  closing 98
  opening 96
wishing plants 95
wishing wells 22, 44, 56, 83–4
world, wish for the 117

Y

the year, wishes for 125
yoga 22

Published in 2021
by Hardie Grant Books,
an imprint of Hardie Grant Publishing

Hardie Grant Books (London)
5th & 6th Floors
52–54 Southwark Street
London SE1 1UN

Hardie Grant Books (Melbourne)
Building 1, 658 Church Street
Richmond, Victoria 3121

hardiegrantbooks.com

British Library Cataloguing-in-Publication
Data. A catalogue record for this book is
available from the British Library.

WishCraft by Shauna Cummins
ISBN: 978-1-78488-349-2

10 9 8 7 6 5 4 3 2 1

Publisher: Kajal Mistry
Editor: Eve Marleau
Design: Evi-O.Studio | Susan Le & Kevin Teh
Illustrations: Evi-O.Studio |
Kait Polkinghorne & Susan Le
Copy-editor: Tara O'Sullivan
Proofreader: Gillian Haslam
Indexer: Vanessa Bird
Production Controller: Sinead Hering

Colour reproduction by p2d
Printed and bound in China
by Leo Paper Products Ltd.

DISCLAIMER

Hypnosis and WishCraft and
the content of this book are
not substitutes for the therapy
and treatment offered by licensed
psychotherapists, counsellors,
psychiatric physicians
or medical doctors.

MIX
Paper from
responsible sources
FSC® C020056